CW00538629

Anatomy of the Ship

The Royal Yacht
CAROLINE
1749

Anatomy of the Ship

The Royal Yacht
CAROLINE
1749

Sergio Bellabarba & Giorgio Osculati

CONWAY

MARITIME PRESS

Publisher's Note

Unlike other titles in the 'Anatomy of the Ship' series *Caroline* was not commissioned specially, but was translated from an existing Italian publication. As a result it varies slightly from the established pattern of the series, notably in the lack of extensive keys to the drawings. However, by way of compensation, the relevant information is contained in a far fuller introductory text.

Frontispiece
1. *Royal Caroline* under sail in a fresh breeze, a detail from the painting by John Cleveley the Elder (c1712–1777) in the National Maritime Museum, Greenwich. *National Maritime Museum*

© Conway Maritime Press 1989

This edition published in Great Britain 1989 by
Conway Maritime Press Limited
24 Bride Lane, Fleet Street
London EC4Y 8DR

First published in Italy as
Royal Caroline (1749)
© *1986 Ugo Mursia Editore*
Milan, Italy

Translated by Anne J Stone

British Library Cataloguing in Publication Data
Bellabarba, Sergio
  The royal yacht Caroline 1749.
  1. Great Britain. Royal yachts, 1740–1800
  I. Title   II. Osculati, Giorgio   III. Series
  623.8'2

ISBN 0–85177–496–2

All rights reserved. Unauthorised duplication contravenes applicable laws.

Designed by Jonathan Doney
Typeset by Inforum Typesetting, Portsmouth
Printed by The Bath Press, Bath

Contents

Foreword

This book has been written principally for makers of ship models. In fact the research which forms the bulk of the material contained here was begun many years ago with the sole purpose of building a model of *Royal Caroline*, with Plate XLIX of Chapman's *Architectura Navalis Mercatoria* as the only available item of information.

In addition to the most detailed plans, we have sought to provide as much information as possible concerning the ship's history and, within the limits of the available space, the contemporary construction techniques and fitting-out procedures, with particular reference to rigging. Given the quality of British specialist publications (recently in particular) on British seamanship and individual ships, it is unusual for foreign authors to venture into a subject like this for such a demanding public. The fact is, however, that once our initial orientation difficulties were overcome, the existence in Great Britain of institutions which are a model of efficiency, such as the Public Records Office, the National Maritime Museum and the Royal Archives, have made our research much easier. We wish once more to express our gratitude to these institutions, as we did in the Italian edition of the book, and particularly to: NAM Rodger of the Public Records Office, DJ Lyon, James Lees and Alan McGowan of the National Maritime Museum.

Finally we wish to explain why we have made some use of the metric system in dealing with a subject like this where the old systems of measurement are still widely used by modelmakers in English-speaking countries. This particularly concerns the thickness of the rigging, which contemporary writers expressed in inches of circumference. We had laboriously converted these to diameters in the metric system for the Italian edition and it seemed a cumbersome and perhaps misleading operation to reverse the process.

References to practices in Continental navies and to the development of rigging were much more plentiful in the text and footnotes of the Italian edition. English language readers have a wealth of specialised works available on this matter which anyone wishing to widen his knowledge of naval history can consult. We will refer the reader to them, but we wish to mention expressly those which we have found most useful in our work, namely *Masting and Rigging of English Ships of War* by James Lees and *Seamanship in the Age of Sail* by Harland and Myers.

Sergio Bellabarba
Giorgio Osculati
Milan, 4 September 1988

Introduction

HISTORICAL BACKGROUND

During the reigns of George II and George III *Royal Caroline* (or *Caroline* as she was more popularly called) was the principal royal yacht. This was a time when England, under the Hanoverian monarchy, was becoming a world power; this meant a sea power.

George II nurtured an almost exclusive interest in the military arts and was the last King of England personally to lead his army into battle (at Dettingen in 1743). His Queen, the energetic, cultured and intelligent Caroline of Brandenburg-Ansbach, took a lively interest in politics, in which she played an important part. This was due to Robert Walpole's esteem for her and her influence over the King, who regularly appointed her Regent when he left for the Continent.

Queen Caroline died in 1737, leaving the King profoundly afflicted. Although the custom of the times allowed him a great deal of licence in his personal relationships, he had always been sincerely attached to his Queen and took no pains to conceal it, much to the amusement of the courtesans.

On his death in 1760, his grandson, 22-year-old George III, succeeded him. George III decided to marry soon afterwards and chose as his bride a very young German princess, Charlotte von Mecklenburg-Strelitz, who became Queen of England at the age of 17.

Charlotte, unlike Caroline of Ansbach, never became involved in politics, and George III, in contrast with his forebears, did not indulge in gallant affairs. The family life of these two monarchs was exemplary in its mutual affection and care for their many children. The thrifty Court habits, the King's invariable good humour and his simple, affable way with everyone created a wealth of popularity and respect which survived the two great tragedies of his very long reign, the American War of Independence and his illness. He governed English politics more directly than this predecessor. He did not personally handle military and naval operations, but he always held the supreme command, and wielded it sensibly. Then, in 1788 and at intervals until 1799, he was afflicted by a form of mental instability which modern pathologists might diagnose as porphyria, a rare hereditary disease. It became chronic after 1810 and a Regent was appointed. Charlotte died, heartbroken, in 1818, bu the King lived on for two more years in ignorance of this.

This is the setting for *Royal Caroline*, built in 1749 and broken up in 1820. These few words on her historical background are necessary because, as will be seen, the events of the life of the ship are intertwined with those of many famous characters. Moreover, she was not only a very beautiful yacht, perhaps the most splendid ever built, but also represented an important stage in the refinement of British shipbuilding. In those days progress was made empirically only, by testing in practical sailing in all weathers the favourable or unfavourable effect of a change made by intuition or arising from the wish to experiment. These changes were usually minimal, but in the very delicate balance which is set up in a sailing ship between the underwater part of the hull and the upperworks, wind force and water resistance, forward movement and leeway, the effects could be considerable and were not always favourable. Numerous experiments were judged failures for one reason or another.

On the other hand it will be seen below that the Admiralty used *Royal Caroline* as the prototype for a long series of frigates of various classes between 1750 and 1800.

It is surprising to find a yacht concerned with the design of warships. The size of *Royal Caroline*, however, was not far from the smallest class of frigate, and it must be remembered that a 'yacht' then was not exclusively a pleasure craft.

A brief note on this type of ship will be a help in understanding these aspects. Some of *Royal Caroline*'s ancestors will be mentioned here, so it will be seen that her qualities as a sailing ship were not a happy accident, but rather the fruit of cautious, almost imperceptible refinements made to the lines of older designs, which had been very successful in the eyes of their contemporaries.

THE DEVELOPMENT OF THE YACHT

The word 'yacht' is Dutch in origin. A small, single-masted, fore and aft rigged craft was termed a *jaght* in sixteenth and seventeenth century Holland. In Dutch and Low German *jaght* meant 'chase' or 'hunt'. This suggests that such vessels were originally used not for peaceful ends, but for privateering. Seventeenth century Dutch writers describe them as excellent sailing craft, fast, very easy to handle and used for ferrying passengers over short distances. Even then the word was often also used to denote a pleasure craft. We know, too, that the Dutch fleet had in its retinue many yachts, whose services were invaluable in exploration, carrying persons or despatches and escorting captured ships into home ports.

It is possible that the term *jaght* referred to different types of ships, though all were characterized by slim lines and ease of manoeuvre. Under the heading 'yacht', Aubin (*Dictionnaire de Marine*, 1702), distinguishes between *speeljagt* and *avisjagt*, that is, between a pleasure craft and a scout. This double meaning continued right down to the eighteenth century, not only in Holland but in England too, where the dual role of the vessel was more marked.

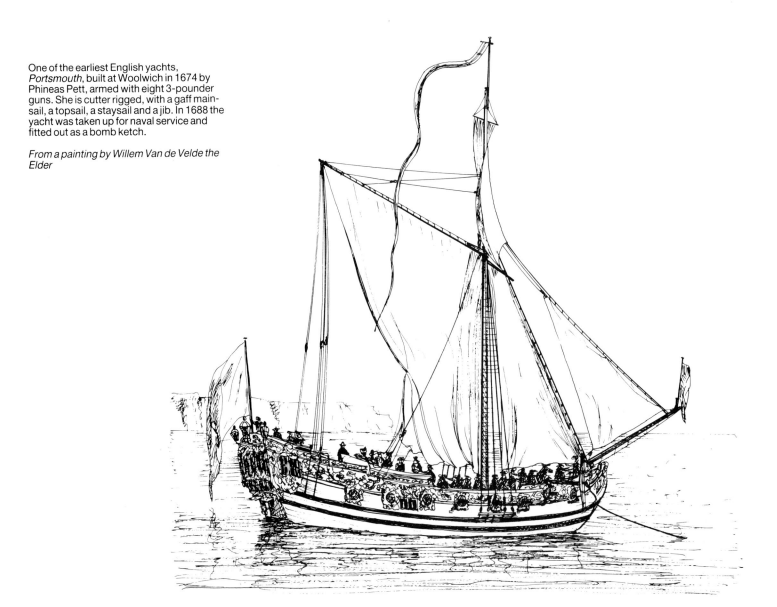

One of the earliest English yachts, *Portsmouth*, built at Woolwich in 1674 by Phineas Pett, armed with eight 3-pounder guns. She is cutter rigged, with a gaff main-sail, a topsail, a staysail and a jib. In 1688 the yacht was taken up for naval service and fitted out as a bomb ketch.

From a painting by Willem Van de Velde the Elder

In those days the distinction between warships and merchant ships was not as clear as it is today. Until the advent of radio communications, every fleet commander needed fast, light vessels to send and receive information and orders. We know what Dutch yachts looked like in the second half of the seventeenth century, which was not much different, we believe, from their appearance during the sixteenth century, apart from the mainsail, which was sprit rigged, since the gaff only came into use around 1630.

There is evidence that yachts were known outside the Netherlands in the late sixteenth century, but their renown is due mainly to Charles II's personal exploits, in contrast to many other small craft developed by the flourishing Dutch navy which never achieved fame outside their home waters. Charles II took refuge in Holland during Cromwell's Commonwealth. There he became familiar with Dutch yachts and yacht racing. During the Restoration he was taken in a Dutch yacht to Scheveningen, where the English fleet waited to escort him home. The King waxed so enthusiastic about this type of ship that

the Burgomaster of Amsterdam asked leave to present him with one, which was renamed *Mary* after the King's sister.

Charles and his brother James made sailing and yachting popular sports in England, betting not inconsiderable sums on their own boats in races.

During this period many yachts were built in England. They were not copies of *Mary*, but more suited to English waters. The Dutch leeboards, flat bottoms and shallow keel, for moving in shallow waters, were abandoned. English-built yachts had a deeper hull and a more marked keel. The first yachts to follow the arrival of *Mary* were named *Catherine* and *Anne*. Both outdid their prototype in speed and seaworthiness, as had been foreseen by their builder, one of the Pett family, in the face of general scepticism. The Dutch immediately responded by producing the small yacht *Bezan* (1661), also presented to King Charles. She defeated both the three earlier vessels and another specially commissioned for the race by the King's brother. Samuel Pepys recorded this with delight as he was not over-fond of English shipbuilders, and particularly not of the Petts.

A ketch-rigged yacht from a painting by
Charles Brooking (1723–1759).

Gradually, bigger yachts were built, with a second mast. This 'ketch' rig was introduced by Phineas Pett (a grandson of the man who built *Sovereign of the Seas*) on *Fubbs*, built at Greenwich in 1682. These craft became so popular that the best naval architects vied with each other to produce them. This was not just a fashionable craze; these same shipbuilders were responsible for designing big warships and the fast cruising vessels later known as frigates. A perusal of the list of yachts built for the Royal Navy from 1660 to 1689 shows that their designers were almost invariably those who were responsible for the two- and three-deckers, the backbone of the English fleet. The list includes Peter and Christopher Pett, the two Phineas Petts (the second and third in this amazing shipbuilding family), Jonas and Thomas Shish, Daniel Furzer and, particularly, Sir Anthony Deane, author of the *Doctrine of Naval Architecture*.

Experimentation to improve the sailing qualities of fast warships thus came largely through yacht construction. They were indeed often confused with ships of the Sixth Rate, which included those armed with twenty or fewer guns. For example, *Greyhound*, built in Portsmouth by Deane in 1672 as a Sixth Rate, 16-gun ship, was long used as a royal yacht. Likewise, many royal yachts were lent to the Navy for normal service at different times.

In Holland during this same period many yachts were built for foreign royalty, following the English style. The plans of some Swedish vessels, (unfortunately rather rudimentary) have come down to us, in addition to various paintings and prints, such as the wonderful *Hyorten* (Deer) painted by Backhuizen in about 1657. Anthony Deane in England supplied Louix XIV of France with two yachts from Portsmouth in 1674–5. There is no evidence that these were ever used personally by the *Roi Soleil*, but it seems that they made a fine sight in Paris, riding at anchor in the Seine.

The accession of William of Orange to the English throne was, however, the end of royal enthusiasm for sailing. The construction of numerous yachts continued nevertheless because of the frequent journeys of court personages between Holland and London. During William III's reign a very special yacht, a distant relation of *Royal Caroline*, was built; it is a curious story and worth a small digression here. In 1698, Czar Peter the Great came to England for three months. Prior to this he had spent some time in Holland, working in a shipyard to acquire practical experience of shipbuilding and a grasp of its theory. His purpose was to learn so as to be able later to impart both theory and practice to his subjects, using his own, highly individual, didactic methods. The English were most anxious for a trade agreement which would give them direct access to the Moscovite markets, and heaped honours on their guest. Among other things, they presented him with a yacht, *Royal Transport*, a model of which still exists in Leningrad Naval Museum. Probably the promise of this gift was one motive for Peter's visit to England. Both the hull and masting of *Royal Transport* were unusual. Her rigging was one of the earliest examples of the schooner type, of which very few seventeenth-century examples exist. The hull was entirely experimental, since her cross section had a slightly concave bottom, a shape only found in Portuguese 'muletas'. This unusual section seems to have been inspired by certain experiments which had been carried out with double hulls in imitation of Polynesian boats. In any case, *Royal Transport* turned out to be perhaps the fastest ship built in England up to that date. Historians of the Russian Navy (which Peter the Great created from nothing) record that she was taken as the model for other ships, but it is not known how many and which these were. She was designed by an amateur, Peregrine, Lord Danby (later the Marquis of Carmarthen), an English gentleman and admiral whose life and adventures were much talked about. He became boon friend and drinking companion of the Czar and was responsible, in no small measure, for the success of the Anglo-Russian trade negotiations mentioned. In 1697 Carmarthen persuaded William III to allow him to design another ship, which was named *Peregrine Galley* in honour of the Marquis himself, as a replacement for *Royal Transport*. Neither the shipyards nor the Admiralty were pleased at the King commissioning the Marquis to design ships; nevertheless, *Peregrine* was exceptionally successful and the Admiralty had no choice but to accept the ship, launched at Chatham in 1700, into its service.

Peregrine was a small 190-ton frigate with twenty small-calibre cannon and a dozen swivel guns. Although she had been originally designed for the Royal Navy, she was often used as a yacht during Queen Anne's reign (1702–1714). We do not know if this was the reason for certain modifications to improve her habitability. In 1714, *Peregrine* was chosen for George I's voyage from Oranienpolder in Holland to Greenwich, to ascend the throne. In 1716 she was officially converted to a yacht and renamed *Carolina*, in honour of the Princess of Wales, and George II's future queen, Caroline of Ansbach.

The original plans of *Peregrine Galley* have not survived, but those of her conversion to a royal yacht still exist. These are the plans of the yacht *Carolina* of 1716. The plans do not give measurements, but these can be calculated from the scale given. The hull between perpendiculars has a length of 86ft 7in (26.47m) and a maximum internal beam of 22ft 6in (6.91m). Depth in hold was 10ft 7in (3.22m). These measurements differ only slightly from those which other sources give for *Peregrine*; (for example, her length is given as 86ft 10in). The small discrepancy can easily be explained by an inexact plan or calculation, so it is likely that the changes made to the Marquis of Carmarthen's

TABLE 1: COMPARATIVE DIMENSIONS OF *CAROLINA* AND *ROYAL CAROLINE*

	Royal Caroline 1749	Carolina 1716
	ft in	ft in
Length of upper deck inside planking	90 1	86 10
Maximum width inside planking	24 0	22 6
Depth in hold at mainframe section (from upper face of keel to upper face of beam)	12 2	10 7
Keel from heel to start of curve of rabbet	72 2½	72 8
Keel from heel to start of cutwater curve	81 4	77 7

Peregrine in refitting her as a royal yacht did not involve the hull, but only the upperworks and internal arrangements. This is all the more likely as *Peregrine* was only 16 years old when she was refitted, and the documents speak of 'refitting', not 'rebuilding' (a euphemism which often masked the construction of a completely new ship). *Carolina* was rebuilt later at Deptford in 1733, and rechristened *Royal Caroline* as George II had succeeded to the throne and Caroline of Ansbach was now Queen. Whether the lines of the 1716 *Carolina* were or were not essentially unchanged from Carmarthen's *Peregrine*, it is interesting to compare them with those of *Royal Caroline* of 1749 and pick out their similarities and differences. The measurements (in feet and inches) of the two ships are given in Table 1.

The ratio between deck length and maximum width inside planking was 3.81:1 in *Carolina*, ex-*Peregrine*. It was 3.75:1 in *Royal Caroline*. Relating the beams to the length of the respective keels also gives similar results, but with the ratios inverted: 3.31:1 for *Carolina* and 3.38:1 for *Royal Caroline*. So *Royal Caroline* had a slightly fuller main frame in relation to overall length and a slightly longer keel in relation to beam. These differences are almost imperceptible, as is borne out by the substantial similarity of the two hulls, but such differences in detail are not negligible. If we look at the longitudinal section of the two ships, we can see that *Royal Caroline*'s stem rises at a more acute angle and is more curved than that of *Carolina*, while her sternpost is nearer the vertical (the rake is 10 degrees compared to 14 on *Carolina*). *Royal Caroline*'s upper deck was considerably higher (about 1ft 5in). The ratio between beam and depth in hold was 2.1:1 in *Carolina* and 2:1 in *Royal Caroline*. The main cabin bulkheads are placed in exactly the same position in the two ships, and even the positions of the capstan and the mainmast coincide. It is obvious that the designer of *Royal Caroline* worked with the plans of the earlier ship in front of him. If we look at the body plan we see immediately that the outline of the main frame is almost identical below the waterline. Forward and aft, however, *Royal Caroline* has sharper lines which are more visually pleasing. It is not known how her designer remedied the resultant loss of buoyancy fore and aft, which would have reduced the seaworthiness of the hull, making it dip into a rough sea instead of riding the waves. Perhaps the balance was re-established by redistributing the weights. The very open V-shaped bottom of *Carolina* became a rounded, more aesthetically pleasing line in *Royal Caroline*. The very strange bell-shaped cross section of *Caroline'a* keel disappeared in *Royal Caroline*. Sections like this were advocated by some authorities (for instance Robert Dudley, in *Arcano del Mare*) during the seventeenth century, though it is surprising to find that such designs were taken seriously. The *Carolina* plan is a builder's document, however, and therefore reliable. When a ship is being

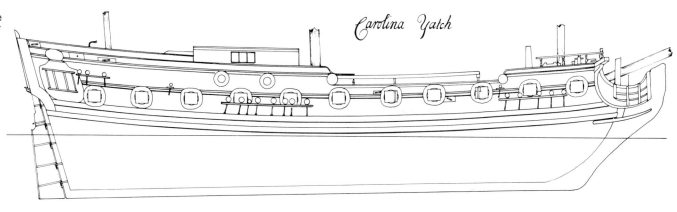

Sheer elevation of *Carolina* (1716), from the plans in the National Maritime Museum. The plans probably show what *Peregrine Galley* of 1700 looked like, apart from the changes to improve her habitability. Designed by the Marquis of Carmarthen, an aristocratic amateur outside the Navy Board's control, *Peregrine* did not have the shortcomings of English light craft of the early eighteenth century.

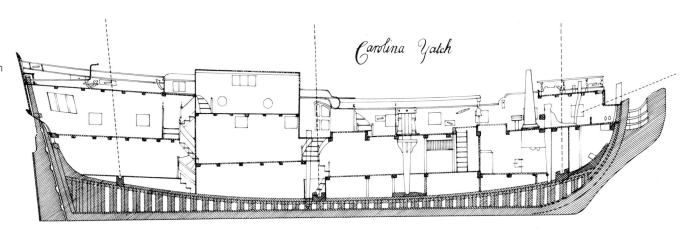

Longitudinal section of *Carolina* (1716), from the plans in the National Maritime Museum.

blown off course, a keel with this sort of section offers greater resistance to lateral movement and is better at countering a tendency to drift. This idea has been taken up again in modern times in giving finned keels to racing yachts. We do not believe that keel sections of the *Carolina* type were still being used on ships built during the eighteenth century. This would seem to confirm that the hull of *Peregrine* of 1700 remained unchanged in *Carolina* of 1716. The *Royal Caroline* keel was 2in (about 5cm) deeper outside the planking by way of compensation.

Royal Caroline's bulwarks slope inwards much less and the chainwales are placed much higher. It is known that Anson had to fight against the opinion of the Navy Board to win this point and change the established rules.

The various companionways to the cabins and the lower deck were simplified on *Royal Caroline*, with a considerable saving in space, particularly around the main mast. This was done to the detriment of the habitability of the stateroom below, which, in *Carolina*, received light and air from two windows onto the main deck, while in *Royal Caroline* it received no light whatsoever.

The 1716 *Carolina* was also luxuriously decorated and had three masts with square sails. Seen sailing in company with the later ship, she would have been difficult to distinguish from *Royal Caroline* but, as we have shown, the two hulls were not completely identical.

CAREER

In 1748 the years were beginning to tell on the old *Carolina* (she had been renamed *Royal Caroline* in 1733, but will be referred to here as *Carolina* to avoid confusion with the later ship). In March that year, the King commented to Captain Molloy that the ship was not exactly in tiptop condition and it was reported to Anson that the hull was in need of urgent repairs.

Her last voyage as a royal yacht took place in November 1748, a difficult crossing from Hellevoetsluis in Holland to Kingsgate, in high seas under reefed topsails. This apparent willingness to set sail, with the King aboard, in all seasons regardless of the weather suggests considerable faith in the seaworthiness of the yacht. After this ordeal, the state of the ship made repairs essential, and the possibility of some improvements was considered.

At this time English shipbuilding was governed by two different bodies with very distinct duties, at least in theory. One was the Admiralty, which was responsible for naval policy and strategy under the King's high command, and therefore decided what shipbuilding programmes were required to achieve political objectives. The other was the Navy Board, a group of technical bodies and administrative offices, which carried out the Admiralty's directives, managed the dockyards, warehouses and the entire ancillary apparatus, designed, built and victualled the ships, decided on their repair or disposal,

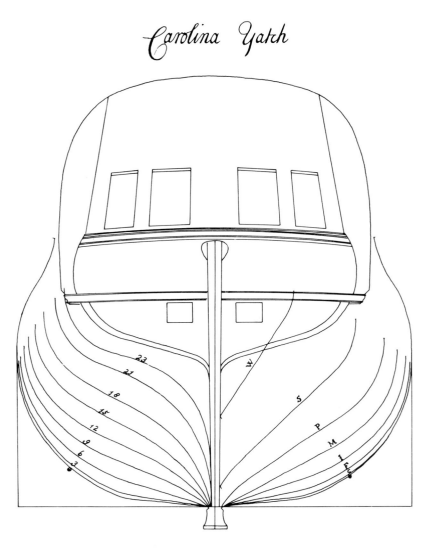

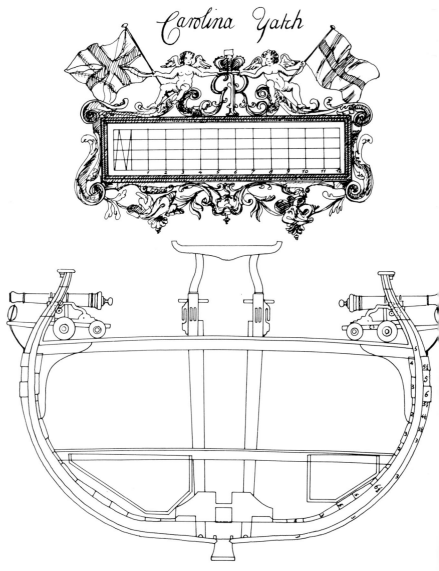

Body plan of *Carolina* (1716). Note the keel section; a section like this is found in the *Arcano del Mare* by Robert Dudley, Duke of Northumberland, exiled to Tuscany around the end of the seventeenth century.

Main frame of *Carolina* from the plans in the National Maritime Museum.

and, not least, defined the financial requirements and administered the funds allocated by Parliament. The Admiralty was made up of political men, usually from aristocratic families, and of high ranking Navy officers seconded to the committee so that their practical experience could guide the other members. Their number varied from seven to nine. Their term of office was not usually long, while on the Navy Board professional technicians of the highest level often spent all their working lives there and jealously guarded their prerogatives and their 'craft'.

Friction between the two bodies was more the rule than the exception. Admiralty orders on matters within its jurisdiction were often loosely interpreted, if not openly ignored. The opposite process also occurred, it must be added in the interests of objectivity, when the Admiralty meddled, sometimes not too happily, in matters that were the business of the Navy Board.

This brief digression is the background to an understanding of the rather curious circumstances which accompanied the building of *Royal Caroline* and to an appreciation of them, especially from a distance of 2½ centuries.

The Woolwich dockyard was asked for an estimate to repair and improve the old yacht. The amount was £2200, not counting regilding the carved decorations. While the Navy Board, whether out of disbelief or undue punctiliousness, asked for the estimate to be reviewed, this time by two dockyards together, the Admiralty cut matters short and ordered a new ship to be built. In a letter dated 26 June 1749, the Master Shipwrights of various yards and the Surveyor of the Navy in person were asked to prepare plans to be submitted for approval by the Admiralty. The new ship, the Admiralty specified, had to be the same capacity and draught as the old one, and would be built according to the best plan from those submitted. Two of these plans have survived, that of

Carolina riding at anchor, from a contemporary painting. Her resemblance to *Royal Caroline* is obvious. *Carolina*, as far as we know, was the first three-masted yacht and the biggest built to date. To judge from some of the rigging details, the painting seems to date from before 1719.

the Surveyor, Joshua Allin, and that of the Plymouth Master Shipwright. It is not surprising that Allin's was chosen, and, objectively, it must be admitted that it was the better. The letter from the Admiralty ordering *Royal Caroline* to be built according to Allin's plans is dated 22 August 1749 and bears the signatures of Anson, Duncannon and Villiers. So *Royal Caroline* was built at Deptford, between London and Greenwich.

Admiralty orders were to build the ship in the shortest possible time, the more so because the old *Carolina* was no longer available for royal voyages. She had been refitted, also in the Deptford yard, as an armed sloop (the smallest three-masted square-rigged naval craft) and returned to the Royal Navy. Deptford had given an estimate of £1494 for this work, advising against it since it was practically the cost of a new sloop, but the Admiralty, in spite of this, ordered them to proceed (letter of 11 July 1749). The actual cost of the conversion was £3331 – a consolation for modern budget planners! The ship

was radically changed after this work (her hull was 3ft longer) and she was renamed *Peregrine Sloop* after her original designer. Her end was tragic: she was lost in the Bay of Biscay in 1762 with no survivors. Originally she was believed to have been captured by the French, as noted in the Progress Book.

Even the birth of *Royal Caroline* was not free from financial disputes; indeed these were lively and hard fought, as we shall see. The shipyard, following the orders of the Lords of the Admiralty, immediately commenced building operations. The Navy Board was responsible for expenditure, however, and since the new craft had not been budgeted for, she had to be financed from what we would now term hidden reserves. The estimated expenditure was submitted only on 26 October. Bearing in mind that a proportion of the carvings, furnishings, panelling, anchors, flags, ballast, and other fittings belonging to the old *Carolina* were to be re-used, the following totals were reached:

Hull, masts and spars	£6137
Furnishings and fittings	£1360
Sculptures	£ 906
Gilding	£1507
Total	£9910

The bill must have been impressive since the total cost of a three-decked, 80-gun ship of the line, for example, was less than £38,000 – fitted out, stored for 8 months and ready to sail. The documents we have been able to consult are not complete, but the impression they give is that the Navy Board did not look too kindly on the new project, while the Admiralty (or more probably Anson in person) was pressing for the new ship to be ready for the beginning of 1750. The Admiralty wrote directly to the Deptford yard, overruling the Navy Board, who retaliated by carping over costs. We shall see in a later section that the Admiralty had other reasons for desiring the new craft besides those of making a new yacht available to enhance the prestige of the King.

Letters passed from the Admiralty to Deptford urging completion, and from the yard suggesting means of speeding matters up (even working during the Christmas holidays was considered). Correspondence between the Navy Board and the yard, on the other hand, concerned the constant stream of high bills to be paid. It is thanks to these disputes over costs that the names of the craftsmen have been preserved, as it was their accounts which caused the disagreements. Heading them is Mr Thomas Burroughs the carver, whose bill came to £1100 11s 0d, a considerable sum. The Navy Board did not wish to undertake the responsibility for paying without confirmation that such a bill was justified. The yard declared that it had no terms of reference to enable it to express an opinion, since the carvings were more numerous and of better quality and finish than on any ship before. The carver was paid his price.

Mr John Bladwell and Mr William Reavour, upholsterers, provided curtains and panels of silk, damask and the finest linens, cushions, upholstery, ribbons, braids and embroidery, amounting to more than £200. The stern lanterns were made by Widow May's company which was the only one to grant a discount, of £2 on the £18 invoiced.

One intriguing item in the fittings is 'Mr Sutton's Air Pipes'. On February 1 1750 the yard asked the Navy Board to send workmen to install these, otherwise they would be unable to proceed with laying the lead ballast. These pipes were part of a primitive ventilation system that conducted hot air from the galley stove to the below-deck spaces in an attempt to prevent rot and decay in the timbers.

The bill for gilding was especially high. Mrs Rosamond Turner's company, the yard explained, 'has laid on with gold size, one hundred and twenty thousand leaves of gold on HMS the *Royal Caroline* in gilding her head, stern and all the frieze and weatherwork fore and aft etc and being the greatest part which is to be gilt for which am humbly of the opinion she deserves to be paid after the rate of 15s for 100 leaves including gold size and workmanship'. This meant another £900. Here the patience of the Navy Board gave out and the curt order to suspend the gilding and painting work arrived at the yard. It was only resumed in July 1750, and with another firm (that of a Mr Stock, who presented a bill of £267 without discount for completing the gilding and painting). It is significant that the carvings were covered with gold leaf, the finest, but by far the most costly, gilding procedure. This was a tremendous luxury, even for those days. The few ornaments on warships received a 'gilding' consisting of a coat of yellow paint with a layer of metal powder applied to it.

The order to build *Royal Caroline* reached Deptford in this letter dated 22 August 1749 signed by Anson, Duncannon and Villiers. The five-month deadline was so that George II could go to Germany in the spring.

From document ADM/A2395 in the National Maritime Museum

Overall the ship cost £12,390, of which £1100, as we have seen, was for the carvings, and £1521 for painting and gilding.

Royal Caroline was launched on 29 January 1750 at 1 o'clock and taken the very same day to the hulks for masting. Her first captain was Charles Molloy, who had commanded the earlier *Carolina*. In February and March, with the furnishings and gilding still incomplete, she was sent for sailing trials along with *William and Mary* and *Fubbs*. The yachts cruised in the Straits of Dover for a fortnight, in variable weather but evidently with generally strong winds, since the logbook frequently mentions sailing under double reefed topsails. Unfortunately, Captain Molloy's report on the yacht's sailing qualities has not survived. This special questionnaire was introduced by the Admiralty about 1743 and had to be filled in by the captain of every ship when first taken to sea; the object was the systematic acquisition of information on the practical success of new types or innovations in design.

When the sailing tests were finished on 8 March, the ship anchored at Deptford. There the Duke of Cumberland, second son of George II and Caroline, visited her, along with Lord Sandwich and a very distinguished company, judging from the titles, which included Princess Amelia, the Duchess of Bedford, the Dukes of Grafton, of Cathcart, and others. It might be said the Royal family took possession of the ship on that day. As early as 17 April the King embarked from Harwich and the ship made the first of a great many crossings to and from Holland (Hellevoetsluis). *Royal Caroline* thus began her career unfinished thanks to the Navy Board's stubbornness over questions of price.

Royal Caroline was used regularly from then on for voyages to and from the Continent. The ports of departure were Greenwich, Harwich and Gravesend, and Hellevoetsluis was one of the principal destinations. From there the King and his entourage proceeded by carriage. On the return voyage, the King usually landed at Harwich, or, occasionally, Margate. The crossing usually lasted one or two days. Depending on the political situation, the convoy of yachts was usually escorted by up to four frigates, largely as a defence against privateers, first French, then Spaniards, Algerians and even Americans during and after the War of Independence. This is why a small yacht like *Royal Caroline* was armed, which in turn explains why an escort of frigates was held to be sufficient. There was always more than one yacht on these royal voyages, in order to house the King's entourage and baggage and so that one could act as galley for the others. The practice of having the King escorted personally by the highest rank in the Admiralty on these voyages was kept up, and the First Lords (Aylmer, Torrington, Berkeley, Anson, Delaware, etc) performed this duty during *Royal Caroline*'s career.

In 1761 the ship was rechristened *Royal Charlotte*, in honour of George III's intended bride. The King's decision to offer marriage to Princess Sophie Charlotte of Mecklenburg-Strelitz in June 1761 had come as a surprise to his Privy Council and consequently the Admiralty was ordered to prepare the ship in all haste to fetch the King's bride-to-be. A yacht named *Charlotte* was renamed *Augusta* to free the name for *Royal Caroline*, which was fitted out in sumptuous fashion at a cost of £5200 – nearly a half of the much-criticised £12,390 for her original construction.

The convoy consisting of the yachts *Mary*, *Katherine*, *Augusta*, *Fubbs* and *Royal Charlotte* set sail on 6 August, escorted by *Nottingham* (60 guns), *Winchester* (50), *Minerva* (32), *Tartar* (28), the sloops *Hazard* and *Lynx* and two cutters, under the overall command of Lord Anson, the Admiral of the Fleet. The return voyage from Stade began on 28 August, and the convoy promptly ran into a major storm. Some of the small craft got into difficulties, and the larger vessels lost spars, but although the convoy was temporarily lost, *Royal Charlotte* was never in any real danger. For Princess Charlotte, who had never been to sea before, it must have been a real ordeal, but she stood up to the week-long buffeting with great spirit. The battered convoy finally arrived off Harwich, to a tremendous welcome, in the evening of 6 September. Like her namesake, *Royal Charlotte* stood up well to the worst of the weather and suffered no serious damage.

During his later years, George III used the yacht for seaside holidays instead of going to Hanover. He regularly went to Weymouth in late August or early September to the residence of his brother, the Duke of Gloucester. Outings in Weymouth Bay were quite rough at times: the cutter *Crescent* broke up on the rocks on 8 October 1804 while escorting one of these outings, and *Royal Charlotte* herself had her spritsail yard washed away by high seas that same month. The ships sailed under reefed topsails only, with, among the other usual precautions, topgallant masts lowered to the deck.

It is not surprising that the King, a keen walker and horseman, enjoyed sailing in all weathers. What is surprising is that the Queen and the princesses did, as can be seen from their private letters. Queen Charlotte was particularly fond of *Royal Charlotte*, especially after the dramatic experience of the famous crossing of 1761, her first experience of the sea. The King abandoned his sea holidays after 1806.

It is worth noting that these voyages by the Royal Family demonstrate how much greater their understanding of Navy problems must have been compared with that of other European monarchs.

A new royal yacht, *Royal Sovereign*, was built at Deptford in 1804; she was slightly bigger than *Royal Charlotte* and perhaps of less pleasing lines. She was also faster than the older yacht. The National Maritime Museum at Greenwich has a lovely figurehead attributed to the *Royal Charlotte* of 1820, a not very successful and short-lived yacht (she was broken up in 1832). This figurehead greatly resembles the young Queen Charlotte, although she had been dead two years when the ship was built, and perhaps was inspired by the figurehead of the original *Royal Charlotte*. The 1869 Catalogue of the South Kensington Museum, where the figurehead was first kept, described it as 'the figurehead of the *Royal Charlotte*, belonging to HM George III' which is clearly impossible since that king was dead before the keel had even been laid. It is possible that this is in fact the figurehead of the earlier *Royal Charlotte*, dating perhaps from 1774, when the carvings and gilding were renovated.

Some brief biographical details of the captains and crews of *Royal Caroline* follow. Her first captain was Sir Charles Molloy, a good sailor but apparently short on ambition. The command of a royal yacht meant for him an honourable and dignified conclusion to a career which had begun in the ranks. It is no accident that most of the captains of *Royal Caroline* were knighted.

Sir Charles Molloy was followed by Sir Piercy Brett, who, according to the surviving logbooks, remained captain until 1757. He probably stayed until 1760, when he assumed command of *St George*. He rose to Rear-Admiral in 1762 and Admiral of the Blue in 1778.

Sir Peter Denis then commanded *Royal Caroline* until 21 October 1770. He, like Captain Brett, had served on *Centurion*, where his career began with promotion to Third Lieutenant by Anson. He left *Royal Charlotte* when promoted to Rear-Admiral and died in 1778 as a Vice-Admiral.

John Campbell was the next, leaving her to command *Victory* with the rank of Rear-Admiral. Then came the most illustrious of all, Sir William Cornwallis, who remained until 1787. He had a fine record in the West Indies and in the Indian Ocean in 1788. Promoted to Rear-Admiral in 1793, he achieved his greatest renown at the blockade of Brest against Napoleon, whose attempt to break the blockade finished disastrously at Trafalgar.

Sir Hyde Parker, who later commanded *Victory* (in 1791), became Rear-Admiral in 1793 and Admiral of the West Indies Fleet in 1799, was next. Captain Henry Trollope followed in 1797, becoming Rear-Admiral in 1801 and Admiral in 1812. Another *Royal Charlotte* captain who became Admiral was Sir Henry Neale, captain from 1801 to 1802. Then came Captain George Henry Towry, who had been lieutenant on the *Victory* under Sir Hyde Parker.

Royal Caroline in a storm. She is lying-to under fore course and mizzen sails. The jibboom has been stowed and the topsail yards lowered to the caps. The main yard has been lowered to the gunwales and the topgallant yards to the deck. The topgallant masts have not however been sent down, probably because it was a risky manoeuvre in a rough sea.

The last captain of *Royal Charlotte* to rise to flag rank (in 1812) was Sir Edward James Foote, captain from 1806 to 1807.

The royal family ceased using the yacht in 1806 and consequently command of the ship lost its appeal for ambitious officers; there are no further famous names among her captains. In her latter days, spent sadly tied up waiting for breaking up, the appointment of her captain must have served to ensure an income for someone in expectation of better things.

Finally, some information remains on the life of the crew. The paybook of *Royal Caroline* for the period from launching (29 January 1750) to 30 June 1750 is kept in the Public Records Office (document ADM 33/414). Captain Molloy's pay for this period amounted to £45 3s 9d. The Surgeon, by the name of Charles Allen, received just less than £27 and the Master, Walter Taylor, just over £21. A midshipman earned about £8 and an able seaman about £6. There were thirty-six seamen, which is double the number of berths since each

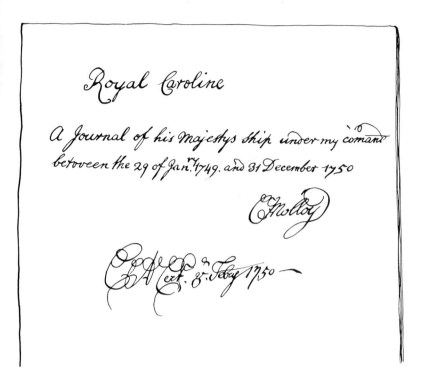

The title page of *Royal Caroline*'s logbook with the signature of her first captain, Sir Charles Molloy.

sailor shared his with a shipmate from the other watch. *Royal Caroline*'s crew had the unusual luxury of bunks, even though they were in the depths of the hold, partly below the waterline. This was probably greatly appreciated by the men from warships who were used to sharing a simple hammock, one of hundreds crammed in tight rows on the gun deck.

The ship's officers, who, in addition to the captain, also lodged in rather spartan fashion between decks, were the Gunner, usually a lieutenant, the Surgeon and the Master. Then there were two midshipmen. The petty officers had even more restricted private quarters which, however, were much envied because they allowed a minimum of privacy for writing a letter, reading, or simply resting. Private quarters, though tiny, were a status symbol. The petty officers who enjoyed these privileges were the Boatswain and the Carpenter. The captain had six servants (lodged in tiny cubby-holes at the far end of the stern) a steward and a clerk. Then there were the other rates who shared cabins in twos or threes, with their own bunk, sea-chest and perhaps a communal table and cupboard. They were the six gunner's mates and the sailing master's three. In all there was provision for seventy men, which corresponds exactly to the paybook and to Captain Molloy's entry in the log (28 February 1750).

Compared to the average English seaman's life of those days the crew of *Royal Caroline* were fortunate. Life was normally peaceful, riding at anchor in Greenwich or Deptford. Every day the Captain read from the Articles (almost always it was the Articles of War) as was the case on board all of His Britannic Majesty's ships. These were portentious clauses threatening floggings and even death for the slightest transgression, but such punishments were not

called for on board *Royal Caroline*. The logbook reports twelve lashes of the cat inflicted on a certain Samuel Jones on 5 March 1766, and that is all.

The logbooks show that maintenance work was a constant necessity, which helped the officers keep the men busy. In all probability the petty officers and the most reliable seamen were given shore leave when off duty, and the chance to check that the local ale was still drinkable and other amusements still available.

When His Majesty decided to use the yacht, she became a hive of activity, with stores loaded rapidly and the other departure preparations swiftly made. Members of the crew were often lent to other ships when they were short due to war or recruiting difficulties. Sir Hyde Parker lent men to *Captain* and *Prince* in 1789 and to *Royal George* in 1790. We can imagine the comments that greeted reinforcements from the royal yacht on these ships which had returned from hard service, or were bound for it.

ROYAL CAROLINE AND THE DEVELOPMENT OF ENGLISH FAST SAILING SHIPS

The eighteenth century saw a new introduction of science into the art of naval architecture. The first attempts to apply mathematical criteria to shipbuilding were made mainly in France. There, mathematics and experimental scientific studies were widespread and traditional shipbuilding methods were not so deep-rooted as in England. There was a French school of physics and applied mathematics engaged in the study of the optimum shape for hulls. Some of the finest scientists of the time were involved; their results, if not brilliant, were certainly a positive contribution.

In the nineteenth century, when this hitherto neglected field of naval history was first studied, it was argued that French ships, based on the calculations of such scientists, were superior, and that the new designs of the traditionally-inclined Royal Navy had only developed by slavish imitation of foreign innovations, especially those of captured French ships. This fallacy is still widespread today. It is true that the Admiralty had the shape and size of captured ships recorded and plans made from them (this was normal in other navies too). It is also true that a fair number of English ships were successfully built on the basis of these plans. Nevertheless, reports on French ships were often far from uncritical.

When it was planned to buy in a captured ship for the navy, a technical commission consisting of representatives of royal dockyards had to decide on the appropriateness of the acquisition, a fair price, the repairs needed and so on. Then, if the prize was purchased, the captain had to make a report on the ship's sailing qualities, as was the case for ships built in England. The captain's sailing quality reports were generally favourable, in some cases almost enthusiastic, but the captains were well able to distinguish between good or excellent performance with calm seas and moderate winds and mediocre or decidedly poor performances in rough seas or at different trims. The best French prize of the 1740s, *Renommée*, was extremely fast (15 knots under full sail) and very handy in coming about, which her captain praised. But she rolled terribly in rough seas and buried her bows in the sea when close hauled with a strong wind because of her over-streamlined bow. *Renommée* aged prematurely and her performance declined rapidly as a result of hogging.

The most detailed criticisms of inadequate building standards come from the dockyard surveys. These reports are agreed on the French ships' lack of sturdy construction; frames were too widely spaced and timbers too light. The number of beams was insufficient and the knees which reinforced the joints between beams and frames were even fewer. The planking was too light and fir

A Journal of the proceedings of His Majesty: ship the Royal Caroline (under my comand) between the 29th of Jany 1749, and the 31. of December 1750.

Remarkable Observations and Accidents

Month and Week Days Jany 1749	Winds	Courses	Dis.	Latde Longde corrected	Ship at Noor	
Munday 29	SWt				Upon the Stocks Deptford Yard	Having recd my Commissn to remove out of the Old ship into the New Royal Caroline rebuilt at Deptford, Accordingly J enterd the usual Complement as before, at 1: afternoon the Ship was Launchd, then J hauld along side the Hulk and set her Masts & Bowspret had moderate galls of wind and fair weather
Tuesday 30	Do				along side the Hulk at Deptd	This afternoon at high water J hauld into the Wet dock had strong gales of wind and much rain
Wednesd. 31	SW to SW				Deptfd wet dock	This morning J began to get in the Lead Ballast and to Rigg the ship had strong gales of wind and fair weather
Febry Thursd. 1	WbW			Do		Strong gales of wind and rainy weather
Fryday. 2	Do			Do		Do
Satturd. 3	Wt			Do		Do with dirty coars weather
Sunday 4	Wt			Do		Do
Mund. 5	Do			Do		Do
Tuesd. 6	Do			Do		Moderate gales, and clear weather
Wednesd 7	NW			Do		Fresh gales, with moist close weather
Thursd 8	SW			Do		Do
Fryday 9	Do			Do		Do
Satturd 10	Do			Do		Do
Sunday 11	Do			Do		Fine moderate gales and clear weather
Mund. 12	Wt			Do		Do
Tuesd. 13	Do			Do		Do
Wednes 14	Do			Do		Bossh gales, and fine clear weather
Thursd 15	WNW			Do		This afternoon J hauld out of the wet dock and made fast along side the Hulk, had smal gales of wind and fair weather
Fryday 16	SW					
Satturd 17	Wt				Long side the Hulk at Deptford	This morning J began to take in our Provisions and fill water, had moderate gales of wind and fine clear weather

The first page of Sir Charles Molloy's log tells us that the ship was launched on 29 January 1749 at 1pm, and was taken the same day for masting.

From document ADM 51/4316 in the Public Record Office

was used too much instead of oak for the upperworks and decks. The fastenings were very poor, consisting almost exclusively of simple iron nails, which were also too few in number, whereas a high percentage of treenails and bolts clinched over roves or locked by a gib were held to be necessary. The Royal Navy, which was notorious for overloading its own more robust ships with armament, was very cautious in this respect with captured ships. At times French prizes were rearmed with lighter guns than they had been carrying when captured, as their structure was judged to be too weak for the weight.

The lightness of French shipbuilding explains their generally good sailing qualities, but also why they aged so rapidly and constantly needed repairs or even rebuilding.

The real situation was that the Royal Navy followed the activities of their traditional adversary with interest, but with no trace of a passive acceptance of their results or a blind admiration of the product of mathematical processes. In construction, the question of accepting French principles was never considered, and as for the lines of the hull, it was a matter of trying to obtain the

Royal Caroline riding at anchor.

advantages of French ships (speed under certain conditions coupled with manoeuvrability) without losing characteristic English strength and sturdy construction. Neither formulae nor theories were capable of providing the complete answers.

Around 1740, the standard smaller English cruising ships comprised two classes: the 40-gun two-deckers and the 20- or 24-gun ships which, strangely enough, were also two-deckers. This latter class had a lower gun deck with only two or three ports, which added little to the ship's fire power, but severely hampered her sailing quality as the upper deck with the majority of the guns was higher above the waterline in consequence. Both the 40-gun ships of the Fifth Rate and the 20- or 24-gun ones of the Sixth were decidedly inferior to their French and Spanish counterparts in size, and generally in performance. The Admiralty was exasperated with the Navy Board's stubborness in defending these types, and indeed was disappointed in the cautious tensions in dimensions made by the 1741 and 1745 Establishments, which failed even to eliminate the most obvious anachronisms like the lower gun deck mentioned

Royal Caroline at anchor while embarking a passenger.

above. In an effort to solve this problem the Admiralty ordered the Navy Board in 1747 to reproduce the hull of a captured French privateer, *Tygre*, without the slighest alteration. This was a ship the Navy had refused to buy because of its weak structure, but it obviously had the lines and handling qualities which the Admiralty could not manage to impose on the recalcitrant Navy Board. At that time George Anson was already at the Admiralty and it would be no surprise if the hand of the energetic captain of *Centurion* lay behind such a drastic order, which certainly was not flattering to the Navy Board.

So, with *Tygre* as model, two 28-gun ships of the Sixth Rate, *Unicorn* and *Lyme*, were built. They can be considered the first two real frigates of the Royal Navy. Not only was the antiquated arrangements of the guns on two decks abandoned, but the lower deck, minus guns and ports, was lowered to the waterline. *Lyme* and *Unicorn* were a complete success and in 1755 the Admiralty ordered two further identical ships, *Lowestoffe* and *Tartar*. At the outbreak of the Seven Years War, many 28-gun ships were ordered, built along the lines of *Unicorn* and *Lyme* and various others of the 32-gun class were also inspired by them. In order to obtain the typical sturdy English construction and to avoid the well-known drawbacks of French designed ships (mainly the

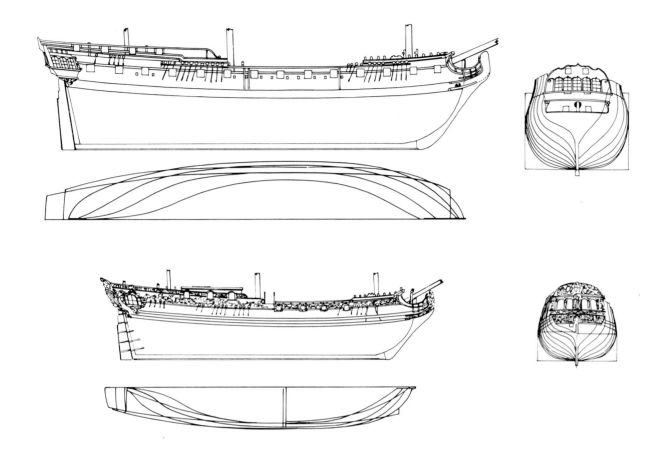

A comparison of the lines of *Royal Caroline* and *Richmond* of 1756, from Robert Gardiner's study of the development of English frigates.

tendency to dip the bows into rough seas), the English plans certainly copied *Tygre*, but not blindly, despite the categoric tone of the Admiralty's order.

At the same time experiments were being carried out on the shape of the hulls of smaller, 20-gun, ships. Two ships of this rate, *Gibraltar* and *Seaford*, were ordered on the same day in 1753. The first was based on *Tygre*, but the second was built along the lines of *Royal Caroline*. This *Seaford* was the first of a long line of ships which included not only 20-gun vessels (*Deal Castle* and *Squirrel* of 1754, and *Glasgow* and *Rose* of 1756), but also bigger and more powerful 32-gun frigates of the *Richmond* class, built between 1757 and 1763 (the class included *Richmond*, *Juno*, *Thames*, *Boston*, *Larke* and *Jason*). The tonnage of these ships was three times that of our yacht, but the hull lines were essentially the same. This was not the end of the story, because in 1804 the Admiralty ordered new 32-gun frigates and once again chose the *Richmond* type. Seven were built, named *Circe*, *Pallas*, *Jason*, *Hebe*, *Thames*, *Minerva* and *Alexandra* – a fine example of the continuity of shipbuilding over a period of time. *Royal Caroline*, launched in 1750, had been based on a late seventeenth century model (*Peregrine Galley*) and designs based on her were being built right into the nineteenth century (perhaps longer, if the truth were known).

Robert Gardiner's very interesting study confirms that French shipbuilding influenced British naval architecture up to a point. On the one hand there was the English shipbuilder's attachment to English building principles based on the strength and durability of the structure. On the other, there was the fact that the best foreign prototypes were used within the terms of a well thought-out, far-sighted policy which sought the best compromise for the real conditions of use: in all weathers, in all seas, under all sailing conditions, with a certain weight of armament, a certain hold capacity for water, victuals and ammunition for many months and (remembering that the Royal Navy served worldwide) a minimum space for lodging the men either in tropical or sub-arctic weathers. Considering all these things, and many others impossible to list here, the problems in making progress in shipbuilding can be imagined, and the reasons for hesitating at innovations and for ignoring mathematical formulae and academic recipes can be understood.

The Admiralty, under Lord Anson, experimented in two directions to obtain a light craft. One was based on a French prize and the other on its own time-honoured national tradition. This is confirmed by Frederik af Chapman, the well-known Swedish naval architect and descendant of an immigrant English naval officer. His famous collection of ship plans entitled *Architectura Navalis Mercatoria* was published in Stockholm in 1769. Chapman had been in England up to 1757 to gain experience in shipbuilding, and he included both *Unicorn* and *Royal Caroline* in his collection, in preference to dozens of other available models, to illustrate a type of light warship or privateer. As a result the only complete plan of *Royal Caroline*'s decorations is now in Stockholm, in the Sjöhistoriska Museum, and it came from the Chapman Collection. Chapman's decision to include both *Unicorn* and *Royal Caroline* in his collection was certainly not arbitrary. On the contrary, he wished to illustrate the two development trends which the Royal Navy was following empirically.

SOURCES USED FOR THE RECONSTRUCTION

Anyone who starts trying to reconstruct (in the sense of faithfully reproducing) a ship no longer in existence would be at a serious disadvantage without a general plan. Our problem was the opposite; three plans of *Royal Caroline* are in existence, all reliable, but not in complete agreement. We obtained two sheets from the National Maritime Museum at the scale of 1/48, copies of the original Admiralty draught deposited at the Museum for the purposes of preservation and study. They show a sheer elevation, an internal profile with the division of the interior spaces, a plan of the upper and lower decks and the hold, a body plan and a half-breadth plan with the waterlines, and a midship section with the outline of the mainframe and the thickness of the planking. It makes not the slightest reference to decoration. Plate XLIX of Frederik af Chapman's *Architectura Navalis Mercatoria* on the other hand shows the decorations in their entirety (at least externally), the sheer elevation with some indication of the interior divisions, the body plan and the half-breadth plan with waterlines and a view of the stern. The Greenwich plans and the plate in *Architectura Navalis Mercatoria* are in agreement, apart from a few details. The most serious discrepancy concerns the deck forward of the beakhead bulkhead, where the knightheads are located. In Chapman's work this deck is higher than in the Greenwich plans. There is also a difference in the shape of the timberheads on the gunwales. Furthermore, the knightheads are omitted altogether on the Greenwich plans. There is a third sheet in the Chapman Collection at the Sjöhistoriska Museum, almost identical to that in *Architectura Navalis Mercatoria*, showing all the decorations. In this the waterlines, diagonals, frames, etc, are extremely carefully drawn and seem to have been studied in great detail. The legend gives the same basic measurements as the Greenwich plan plus the displacement (9443 cubic feet) and a table of the dimensions of the masts and spars to which we shall come back later.

So far this is a slight basis for reconstructing the rigging. Fortunately there is a fourth source, not technical, but from the hand of an artist. This is John Cleverley the Elder's painting of the ship under sail on the larboard tack in a fresh breeze (see Frontispiece). Cleveley's technical competence can be judged from the fact that he was originally a shipwright – in the very dockyard at Deptford in which *Royal Caroline* had been built. The photographic accuracy of his 'portrait' is evident if the details he illustrates are compared with those in the plans. It is therefore reasonable to suppose that he has reproduced no less accurately those details that are not shown on the surviving plans. These include the entire masting, and a deal of other information to be found nowhere else, such as the form of the main bulkhead and its ornament, the positioning of the boat and its appearance, the existence of three stern lanterns, a glazed companionway, decorations inside the stern bulwarks and so on. Cleveley indicates the existence of four carved gargoyle scuppers per side which were not included in any of the plans mentioned, as if such small details were too trivial.

Auxiliary sources are the various documents on the ship's construction (bills, correspondence, etc) mentioned in the other sections and, for the masting and rigging, those sources listed below. *Masting and Rigging of English Ships of War* by James Lees has been used particularly extensively for reconstructing the rigging.

The order of priority has therefore been, for the hull, the Admiralty draught from the National Maritime Museum, complemented by John Cleveley's painting. Where these differed from the *Architectura Navalis Mercatoria*, the Admiralty plan has been followed. The decorations follow strictly those of the *Architectura Navalis Mercatoria* drawing, which correspond almost completely with the Sjöhistoriska Museum plan. All the details which it has been possible to deduce from the painting by Cleveley have been used. We have taken the dimensions of the masts and spars from contemporary Royal Navy regulations. The tables in the Stockholm plan give much taller masting (about 10 per cent). It is possible that *Royal Caroline*, as a royal yacht, was masted differently from what was then considered the optimum for a warship of her size. There is, however, no mention of this in the sources although they do go into fairly substantial detail. We finally decided not to use the tables contained in the Stockholm plans when a projection from Cleverley's painting corresponded almost perfectly with normal masting dimensions of English ships midway through the eighteenth century; for us this was decisive evidence.

We based the rigging almost entirely on James Lees's work, here too favouring Cleveley when they differed. For more minute detail, such as the thickness of cordage, the types of ropes, the shape of rigging accessories, we relied largely on David Steel's *Elements of Rigging*.

The description of the ship is principally through the drawings, in which we have tried to illustrate practically every detail. We have restricted ourselves to a few comments, at times explaining the function of a particular fitting or the reason for a given arrangement when it was not immediately obvious. In other instances details on the materials used in shipbuilding, or the date when a certain feature was introduced, are given. We have done our best to resist the temptation to digress into the history of shipbuilding, and be led away from our specific subject.

HULL STRUCTURE AND PLANKING

The building of big wooden hulls with load-bearing frames reached a stage in development at the end of the sixteenth century in which all structural elements were already present more or less as in nineteenth century ships. So refinements were slow in the seventeenth and eighteenth centuries. Building methods varied from country to country only in the details. All ships, or at least all square rigged sailing ships which were built in European shipyards from Trieste to Königsberg, were essentially the same from a structural point of view.

Eighteenth century English shipbuilding is fairly well documented, first by a number of original contemporary models made by the dockyards which had built the ships. Then there is a considerable amount of modern, high-level, research. What is missing are systematic, detailed works by contemporary writers during the early eighteenth century. These were only produced at the end of that century.

Since the plans of *Royal Caroline* provide many indisputable elements, we can hope that the hull structure described below is, if not identical, at least very close to the original.

She was certainly built like the other ships of the time. Correspondence shows that she received greater attention than was usual for a small vessel of the Sixth Rate. She was a small ship and many structural elements which had to be made up from several timbers on large ships could easily be made from a single plank or tree-trunk for her.

The longitudinal structure, formed of keel, false keel, keelson, sternpost and stem, is clear from the drawings. Here we would observe that the keel was built of elm in several pieces joined by vertical scarphs, while the oak keelson and false keel were fashioned from several pieces joined by horizontal scarphs. A minimum of six or eight metal fastenings joined the two elements at each scarph joint and long bolts ran upwards from the lower face of the keel, through the individual ribs to the upper face of the keelson, where they were clinched over roves. These bolts did not pass through the false keel, which was joined to the keel by staples and by nails hammered in upwards from below. In this way the whole framework did not need to be dismantled to replace a damaged false keel. If the ship ran aground, the false keel broke easily because of its weak joint with the keel and in a certain sense acted as a 'shock absorber' to the body of the ship.

The metal bolts, which were distinct from nails, ran through the whole thickness of the pieces to be joined and were clinched at the opposite end from the head. They were round bars, up to 2 inches thick on large ships, with a truncated conic head which was countersunk in or, sometimes a rounded head which protruded from, the wood. The craftsmen who did the job of inserting these bolts or rods through the wooden skeleton were highly specialized, and this was their sole occupation. It seems incredible today that, using only hand drills, they could cut a passage through a solid wood bow or stern more than 9 feet thick with minimal deviation from true.

Ordinarily the bolts were made of iron or a copper alloy. Iron, under moist conditions, reacted in contact with tannic acid (in which oak is particularly rich) and caused the metal to corrode rapidly and the wood to decay. Nails and bolts soon ceased to be watertight and the joints loosened. So there was a tendency to make them in a copper alloy, which was less resilient than iron but much more durable in seawater. This became the rule when the practice of coppering the hull was adopted in England between 1770 and 1780.

Bolts subject to particular tensile stresses (for example those which fixed the knees at the ribs and beams), rather than being clinched over a rove, were fixed with a key or metal spike called a 'gib' which fitted into a hole running diametrically through the bolt itself, resting against a rove. The entire skeleton of the ship was held together by these bolts, while nails were used only to join pieces less subject to stress.

The athwartship structure consisted of frames usually formed by a pair of ribs bolted together. Every third pair is shown in the Admiralty plan. The frames were composed of different pieces since it was not possible to find wood of a suitable length and curvature naturally. In three-deckers, each rib might have been formed of seven or nine pieces. In *Royal Caroline*, as can be seen from the main frame taken directly from the original plans, it was formed of only five parts, a floor timber and two futtocks per side. Naturally, the joints between these elements were in different places in the two ribs which formed the frame so that when the two ribs were joined by the bolts, the result was a fairly rigid whole. Drawing B1 shows the English method of building frames around 1750.

The 'room' or distance between the timbers was very narrow in ships of the line. The tendency was for it to be less than the calibre of enemy shot, at least up to the gun deck. Higher up, as the section of the futtocks reduced, the space widened. Light craft were built according to less expensive criteria, leaving wider spaces between the frames. The original *Royal Caroline* plans show that the room was more or less the section of a frame.

Ballast, in the form of lead slabs, was placed in the interstices between the floor timbers. Normally there was little or no space between the floor timbers of warships and the ballast, in the form of cast iron slabs, old cannon balls or simply gravel, was laid above the internal planking. The system used on board *Royal Caroline* left more free space in the hold and this, as can be seen from the longitudinal section of the ship showing the internal divisions, was exploited down to its last cubic metre. Stowing the ballast in the lowest possible position made for greater stability, and also made it easier to keep the bilges clean and prevent an unpleasant odour from fouling the air below decks. This was,

however, a peculiarity of this ship, not to be taken as a general rule. Among other things, a centre of gravity very much below the centre of the hull due to the special lead ballast gave the ship much greater stability, but after being heeled over by a gust of wind or a wave, her righting was much faster and sharper. The masts were stressed more and even the hull structure felt the effects. Hutchinson (*Practical Seamanship*, 1777) dwells at length on this subject with illuminating examples. Cargoes that were too heavy and compressed were not to be stored below the estimated hull centre to avoid the risk of the topmasts breaking off as a result of rolling too quickly. In *Royal Caroline* this drawback could easily be corrected by adjusting the amount of ballast so as to give a stable ship without excessive 'stiffness', and an uncluttered hold for personnel and equipment. Hutchinson's work makes interesting reading because he displays his very fine intuitive appreciation of the forces governing the movements of a hull in water.

With regard to materials, the entrenched Royal Navy opinion was that British oak was by far the best type of wood. Hard, compact, durable in seawater as long as it was well seasoned, it was excellent timber. But some of the various species of Mediterranean oak were just as good and the magnificent woods which the Spaniards used in their shipyards of Manila and Havana were even better – alas, only as long as the forests lasted!

All *Royal Caroline*'s planking (decks included) was of English oak. This gave the hull the warm, yellowish-brown colour seen in many marine artists' paintings. The planking consisted of strakes 10 to 12 inches wide, about 3 inches thick for a small ship (7 to 8cm). Planks a little narrower tended to be used for the decks as they were less subject to structural strain, and thus to splintering. The planking was fixed to the hull frame using nails, bolts and treenails. There is a certain amount of confusion on this point due to the inaccuracy of certain authors, who lump periods, national traditions and types all together. The practice in England around the middle of the eighteenth century was to use treenails for a good part of these fastenings. This combined the advantages of economy (compared to iron and copper alloys), lightness and durability. They neither oxidized nor corroded the wood into which they were driven, and lasted practically as long. It is obvious that at the beginning the resistance of an iron nail or bolt was much greater than a treenail, but after two or three years the situation was the opposite.

The following is one possible method for fixing the planking: two treenails for each strake on every frame, and two metal bolts running through and clinched on a rove at every butt joint between planks in the same strake. A metal nail was interposed in every two or three frames. When the width of the strake was less than 9 inches (20cm), a single treenail was used on each frame. Metal nails only were used on the wales and they were bigger and more numerous than those on normal planking. They were often round-headed instead of flat.

The deck planking was fixed to the beams by treenails alone. Since there is often discussion on this point we would say that these treenails must not be confused with the dowels which were (and still are) used to cover the heads of bolts fixing deck planking to the iron frame of composite hulls, or the heads of spikes which attached planks to wooden beams where this was the practice. The grain of the dowels ran parallel to the deck, both for aesthetic reasons and because the deck had to remain uniformly smooth in use. These problems obviously did not arise with treenails. There were two treenails for each beam and ledge per plank. The diameter of the head was 1½ to 2 inches (3 to 4cm). The deck was fashioned from planking running parallel to the keel for the whole length. The habit of tapering planks at the extremities of the decks was not unknown in the Royal Navy but the above rule applied more frequently.

The planks were always jointed regularly on a beam, with an interval of three or four strakes between joints on the same beam. Caulking between the strakes was done with oakum and pitch which gave the seams between the planks, about one centimetre wide, a dark grey or blackish colour.

DECORATIVE WORK

Many ornamental ship carvings have survived from the age of sail. They are few in terms of the vast number produced, considering that every ship, of whatever size and however modest, was entitled to some form of decoration. The quality of the surviving works is generally good and a few examples are above average, finely made and displaying a high level of plastic expressiveness. It is only prejudice which denies them their rightful recognition as genuine works of art.

A ship's figurehead or carved frieze was rarely accorded the same fate as a church statue, choir stall or bas-relief. Where these latter have often found their proper places in museums, the former generally ended up in the breaker's yard as firewood. The *Royal Caroline* carvings were carried out, as we have seen, by one of the most esteemed artisans in this field. We believe that they were of excellent quality, both from the express recognition accorded him by the dockyard in its correspondence with the Navy Board, and because of the particular commitments that a work of such prestige would have imposed on any artist. Chapman's drawing reflects this impression of high quality. It was probably taken from the artist's design, very likely to scale (we do not think that Chapman's drawing was taken from life, that is, from the finished ship). The carvings certainly represented a very fine example of eighteenth century high relief: delicate, pleasing and perfectly finished.

We have done our best to reproduce them in every detail in the illustrations, without omitting or adding anything to what is shown in *Architectura Navalis Mercatoria*. The groups and the single figures are inspired by classical mythology, in keeping with the taste and culture of the times. Now only a few can easily be identified by their more obvious attributes, such as Jove's thunderbolts, Juno's geese and Neptune's trident. There is little to add to what is evident from the drawings. Judging from contemporary models of ships decorated with carved reliefs, we have estimated that at no point was the relief higher than 4 inches. The wood used cannot be identified from surviving documents. The letter of 24 August 1749 from the dockyard to the Navy Board, dealing with the old *Royal Caroline*'s carved work, side panels and carlings for use on the new ship, mentions mahogany, though not necessarily for the carvings.

We would like to dwell a little longer on one point which seems particularly important. This is the way in which the figurehead is presented in *Architectura Navalis Mercatoria*. We have said that our reconstruction faithfully follows this source; we have been obliged, however, to make an exception for the figurehead. Chapman's reliability is beyond question, but we have serious doubts as to whether his representation of the figurehead can be taken literally.

He shows a figurehead whose principal figure is not directing its gaze in the direction of the ship's keel but is looking to starboard, that is towards the observer, while a putto, however pretty he may be, is obscuring her view in the direction of, and turning his back to, the ship's course. From the front, the putto's back dominates the composition.

Seen from the right, the group is not without its charm, but seen from the left and from the front it does not seem to conform to the aesthetic taste of the period, nor to the standards of the ship herself, in which no other detail so discordant can be found.

The figurehead of a ship was not merely an ornament. Seamen generally regarded a ship as a magical, almost human, entity, with her own destiny, which was bound up with that of the crew. Sailors still regard ships this way up to the present, and many true sea stories bear witness to the strength of this feeling, for example in the case of captains voluntarily going down with their ships. These sentiments were concentrated and embodied in the figureheads. Each ship of the age of sail which had a figurehead, however modest and rudely carved, belonged to that world.

This is the context of our instinctive reluctance to accept the composition of the *Royal Caroline* figurehead group as represented by Chapman. We asked ourselves if there was not some way of reconciling respect for such an authority with the fact that no known figurehead is composed like the *Mercatoria* version. The plans which are currently at Greenwich do not show the carvings which appear in the Swedish work which was published in Stockholm in 1768. Chapman's source is probably the same drawing that he obtained, perhaps illegally, from England. This drawing (catalogued under number 1731 in the Sjöhistoriska Museum) follows the one in Greenwich almost exactly. The small differences in detail do not seem to derive from mistakes in copying, but rather to changes made to the plans at the last moment. The drawing does not include the internal divisions, which appear in detail in the Greenwich plan and which are included, if somewhat summarily, in *Architectura Navalis Mercatoria*. This would suggest that Chapman used two plans: a copy of the one whose original was left in England, without the carvings, but with the internal partitions; and an original with the carvings, but only the external view, which is in Stockholm. But drawing No 1731 in the Sjöhistoriska Museum, which was done by an anonymous draughtsman in an English dockyard, must have had some source for the carvings. In our opinion, this can only have been the carver's own design sketch. We saw in the correspondence between the dockyard and the Navy Board, that there had been an estimate for the cost of gilding, and this estimate must have been based on a design which showed the amount of carving to be covered in gold leaf.

We believe that the carver's drawings would have shown the main groups fully in the round and in perspective to give a clearer idea. This would have meant one or more front or three-quarter views for the figurehead. Instead, drawing No 1731 showed the ship as was the normal practice in shipyard plans, which contained a sheer elevation and – but not always – a stern view. Drawings showing a frontal view of the bows are rare. One can surmise that the unknown draughtsman who added the ornamentation had used a sort of false perspective, showing in side view what in reality was covered by the main figure – that is, the implausible putto – since presenting the plan using the usual dockyard convention (ie with a single side view) would have made it impossible to show what was behind the main figure in the group. Following these theories, we decided to present the figurehead differently from the drawing in the *Mercatoria*. To our mind it is the only satisfactory arrangement from the aesthetic point of view and puts the figurehead in perfect harmony with the traditions of this art form.

We have attempted to give some idea of the internal arrangements in the plan and longitudinal sections, though these reconstructions are not based on actual evidence. In the history of the ship given above we have mentioned various letters dealing with the supply of furnishings and ornaments for the cabins, the works of painters, etc, but there are no other clues apart from the material used: damask, mahogany and silk. We have, however, given an impression of one way in which the space (ample by modern standards) could have been used.

The interior decks have inlaid decoration. A certain amount of evidence exists for this, notably in models in the National Maritime Museum. The interior of *Fubbs* is particularly beautiful, with an elaborate inlay on the decks of lilies and multi-pointed stars and panels painted pale blue and yellow; these were colours extensively employed for decorative purposes during the eighteenth century.

COLOUR SCHEME

Our information on the colouring of the hull and the upperworks is drawn, for the most part, from a careful examination of Cleveley's painting. The ship's underwater hull was painted with white antifouling, which must in fact have been closer to off-white. The sides were a natural oak colour, apart from the two wales which were painted black. The colour of the oak from which these ships were made darkened in time since a mixture of vegetable oil, turpentine and resin was applied for protection. The colour of the planking in Cleverley's painting, however, is rather light, rather yellow than brown. Above this was a decorative moulding, interrupted by the gunports and by the quarter galleries. This was gilded on a black ground.

Similarly coloured were the curved rails and the cheeks which supported the timbers of the head and finished with an upward sweep, at the feet of the principal figurehead statue. The figurehead group, in the round, was completely gilded. Then came the large frieze with carved figures, gilded on a light blue ground. In those days a shade of blue close to turquoise was commonly used for decoration, and this would seem to be the shade which appears in Cleveley's painting.

Above this was another scrolled moulding, gilded on a black ground, then a series of rectangles beneath the gunwales, in gold on a pale blue ground. The gunwale was black. The short stanchions supporting the rail from the forecastle to the steps on the bulwark were black and their carvings gilded. The beakhead bulkhead repeated the colour scheme of the sides.

Cleveley is not the source of information for the stern view but we have no doubt that it followed the same general scheme. The lower part of the stern was in natural wood, while the section above it on either side of the rudder hole was probably painted rather than carved (this can be deduced from the different style in which this part is drawn in *Architectura Navalis Mercatoria*). The window section of the stern was mainly black, with the various carved figures gilded, while the top part beneath the taffrail continued the blue ground of the main frieze along the sides. It is not known if the coat of arms in the centre of the stern decoration was gilded or painted.

The gunports were framed by gilded putti while the sides of the gunports were red, like the inside of the bulwarks themselves. The midships bulkhead was red with gold carved decoration. The royal coat of arms in the centre of this bulkhead is our invention: Cleveley's painting does not give details as fine as this. According to contemporary practice, we think that natural wood was used for the hatch coamings, the gratings, the bitts with their crosspieces and the pump. The gun carriages were natural wood colour or red. The capstan was red with, perhaps, the band round the head with the slots for the bars, black. The colourings of the masts will be dealt with in the chapters on rigging.

While we are on the subject, a few words on the colours of old ships in general might be useful. The paints available could be mineral-based like the various earths containing pigments, or organic, as in vegetable extracts. We know that from Greek and Roman times it had been possible to make all the colours in the rainbow in all shades, including the most subtle and brilliant. This is borne out by paintings from classical and medieval times, which contain colours which are splendid if small-scale. But could they be used at sea? Colours had to stand up to salt water and, given the vast areas to be covered, also had to be fairly economical. This drastically limited the available colours, much more so than is generally understood.

An article dealing specifically with this subject has recently been published in the German magazine *Das Logbuch*. What we know of the methods for obtaining the various colours, and the dates when new procedures were invented, suggest that the choice was indeed restricted. White with a lead carbonate base was available from earliest times, and the same can be said about yellow, obtained from fairly common earths containing hydrated iron oxides from which ochre-hued pigments were produced (but not the other colours which nowadays are grouped in the yellow range). There were various possibilities for red at a more-or-less reasonable price and it can be said that a good range of colours was available for nautical use. Blue was the most difficult colour and right up to the start of the eighteenth century there was no practical possibility of decorating ships using this colour. The semi-precious stones which were ground up at exorbitant prices to obtain the wonderful colours in paintings and miniatures (lapis lazuli, turquoise, acquamarine) were mostly unsuited to making a paint which was resistant to seawater. Indigo-based colour, on the other hand, when mixed with oils to make paint, lost its lovely hue and became blackish and unattractive. This situation changed only after 1704, the year in which 'Prussian Blue' was synthesized in Berlin. It was a dark blue with an iron chloride base which, when mixed with white clay, could provide all the shades of blue at a low cost. There had been problems for green too, before the invention of Prussian Blue (which could be mixed with yellow ochre to give any shade of green). The colour which had been available before, obtained from verdigris, did not give either a wide range or very pure colours. Other mineral-based earth colours in the green range were very costly and tended towards olive. Black however was no problem, because lamp-black (which is still widely used today in the chemistry of colourants) gave an excellent stable pigment at a low cost.

Clearly then, not all the colours which appear on models and in paintings really decorated the ships which they depict. Fortunately, *Royal Caroline* was built in an age when shades of blue were not only fashionable, but also both available and practical.

FITTINGS

The capstan. The capstan was one of the few mechanical means available on old ships for reducing the crew's physical labour. Apart from handling the anchors, it was used to hoist and lower masts, to lower yards to the deck, to take aboard boats and guns and, in general, for all the so-called 'all-hands' operations for which the strength of every man who could be put to heave on a rope did not suffice. The capstan consisted of a barrel pivoting inside a step which, in *Royal Caroline*, stood on the bottom of the hull. On the upper deck the barrel rotated freely inside stout partners lined with an iron bush. Above the deck the capstan was fitted with vertical ribs known as whelps. These were set into the barrel and held in place by strong iron bolts, and gave a better grip on the rope which otherwise would have slipped on the smooth barrel. The whole was reinforced by two sets of chocks, one near the head and the other near the base of the capstan, and these slotted into the whelps. A clearly defined method was required to assemble a capstan since each piece had to lock into the others. The head consisted of two superimposed wooden discs with the grain of one at right angles to the other. They were held together by the usual clinched bolts. The underside of the head carried the mortices for the heads of the whelps and the barrel, which ended in a square or octagonal tenon. Moreover, the head carried the slots for the bars with which the crew turned the capstan. At times the head of the capstan was finished with an iron ring which could be decorated in relief. We have used a very simple ornament in our design, but there do exist models of elaborately carved capstans.

The plan of the capstan shows small round holes in its head, centred on the slots for the bars. Pins for keeping the bars in position while in use were passed through these holes. Some illustrations of later periods show these pins attached by a chain to the underside of the capstan head, but we do not think that this was usual in 1750; indeed we are even doubtful whether the use of pins for holding the bars in position was regular practice. They were held together by a swifter (a light cord) which was run right round through eyebolts, or holes at the outer ends of the bars, and pulled taut on itself to prevent the bars from coming loose.

There was a simple locking device at the base of the capstan. In this case it consisted of two metal pawls pivoting on a bolt which could secure the capstan by locking into one of the whelps. A ship's boy, slipping between the sailors who were heaving on the capstan, operated these pawls by hand when commanded by the petty officers in charge. This was no insignificant task; when certain manoeuvres requiring all hands were carried out (for instance attempting to free a fouled anchor) the pawl might get no purchase, or break under the strain, and the resulting sudden backlash of the bars when the ship rode a wave could kill a seaman. In earlier times these pawls were formed of a single very wide V-shaped piece which could engage a whelp in one direction or another as desired. In later times the system changed and two drop pawls suspended from the capstan chocks engaged on a circular toothed crown and automatically prevented it from turning in the other direction.

The *Royal Caroline* capstan barrel, as noted above, ran right down to the bottom of the hold. On the orlop deck the capstan could be used to handle the mooring cables, which could be laid out from the two stern ports. Bulkheads between the capstan and the stern were probably fitted with a fairlead to let the cables pass.

Ground tackle. On the small forecastle of *Royal Caroline* were two large, rectangular spanshackles attached to the deck by two eyebolts. These devices were used for handling the anchor in combination with a large beam called the fish davit. When required, this davit was inserted into the spanshackle and placed in the appropriate recess on the side. One third of the davit's length projected over the side carrying a large single block through which ran a stout cable. At one end of this cable was a hook big enough to catch the anchor around its shank. The other end of the cable carried a tackle made of fiddle blocks. The tackle was hooked to an eyebolt on the main deck, while the runner went to the capstan.

Weighing the anchor took place in three stages. First it was raised from the bottom using the capstan and hoisted until its ring reached the hawse hole. The anchor cable itself was too thick to pass round the capstan; instead the more flexible messenger was used in this operation. When the anchor reached the hawse hole, it was catted, that is raised by the cat tackle, until the ring was level with the cat davit. Then, using the fish davit, it was laid with the shank horizontal between the cat tackle holding the ring and the fish tackle holding the anchor by the throat (the junction between shank and arms). At this point, if the anchor was to be made fast on the chainwales, the cat tackle had to be slackened a little so that the anchor moved aft, until the desired position was reached. If it was to be made fast to the ship's side immediately aft of the fish davit, the cat davit was not slackened. The foretackle, another tackle which

was worked from the foremast head, came into action to move the anchor on board. The anchor was finally made fast to the hull, using chains or cables called shank painters to lash it to the timber heads, which were ranged along the rail.

The anchors of large ships were a product of the blacksmith's art. The largest were 16 to 20 feet (5 to 6m) in length, weighed several tons, and were, without comparison, the largest man-made iron objects before the industrial age.

In the eighteenth century ships usually carried two or four anchors of an adequate weight and these, although they kept their different names, were the same size or two different sizes. The two smaller anchors were usually kept at the cat davit, and the two larger on the chainwales.

The anchor cable, raised as described, passed through the hawse hole and the weed and slime were roughly cleaned off: it then passed through the manger, a triangular area at the extreme bows, closed by a bulkhead. Some of the water which the cable had absorbed drained off on this bulkhead. Then it passed into the depths of the hold where it occupied a lot of space. The cable tiers to take these bulky items usually had gratings for the water to run off into the bilges and to air the cables.

Deck fittings. The hatchways were normally covered with light wooden gratings. There were various types of these, with square or rectangular holes, on eighteenth century ships. Judging from the best original eighteenth century models, the gaps could measure from 2 to 3 inches (5 to 8cm). They were certainly bigger on seventeenth century ships. Gratings allowed the lower decks to be ventilated, as well as providing passageways and working surfaces for the crew. In bad weather the hatchways were made watertight in various ways. The closure had to withstand pressure in both directions, since, when a wave breaks on a hull, which is always slightly elastic, the pressure increases inside it and would make the hatchcovers pop out like corks from a bottle unless they were firmly held in position.

On *Royal Caroline*, one of the after gratings had two holes to let the anchor cables through. These holes were stopped with wooden wedges and sealed with rags or oakum so that water could not penetrate the cracks. Under particular trims, with a rough sea and the wind abeam, the decks of small ships were constantly awash to the gunwales as the scuppers could not drain them fast enough, which is why all openings on the deck were so carefully sealed.

The mast partners were also made watertight. The partners were usually greater in diameter than the mast. When the mast was fitted with stays and shrouds and finally fixed at the proper rake, the remaining space in the partners was closed with specially made, softwood wedges which left no gaps. The wedges were then covered with a tarred canvas, which was attached to the deck with flat-headed nails and lashed to the mast with rope. At times the lashing and cloth were removed so that the wedges could be knocked out from below with a mallet. This was sometimes done by captains seeking the best possible speed out of the ship, since it was generally accepted that an advantage was gained by giving the mast some play in the partners.

Lanterns. The plan in the National Maritime Museum includes a simple drawing of a stern lantern. Cleveley's painting shows that the ship had three lanterns, so we have taken the two side lanterns from the centre one, making them smaller. The size of the yacht lanterns was fairly restricted (20-inch glass panel for the biggest) and this suggests that they were made of iron like ordinary land lanterns. This supposition is confined by the fine brackets in the plans mentioned, which could only be made in iron. Big ships' lanterns, into which several people could fit, were mainly made of wood. The forward wall of the lantern was blind, made of wood or iron sheeting, in order to prevent the lantern light from dazzling the helmsman or those on the night watch. We have placed a smaller lantern on the main top. This detail comes from a painting showing *Royal Caroline* in 1761, at the time of the voyage to Germany.

THE SHIP'S BOAT

The only available source for reconstructing *Royal Caroline*'s boat is Cleveley's painting, which shows a rather large craft positioned on the main deck, in the usual manner for eighteenth century ships, which lacked gangways between the quarterdeck and forecastle. The main topsail sheet bitts were extended vertically so that a crossbeam, called the boat gallows, placed on them was on a level with the forecastle deck. The spare masts and spars which every ship carried rested on this beam at one end and on the forecastle deck at the other. They usually consisted of a main and fore topmast and a lower yard for each of these masts. In addition two squared timbers were often carried so that they could be used for either a yard or a mast. The stock was completed by various minor spars. These pieces of masting were lashed in two bundles, one to starboard and one to port, and the ship's boat rested on these. A cushion of old sails was placed between its hull and the wood and the whole made fast in good seamanlike fashion. The boat which Cleveley shows us was certainly arranged in this way.

The boat is surprisingly large; the distance from the mainmast to the forecastle is about 27 feet (8m). This was a typical size for launches on warships, which were bigger than *Royal Caroline*. Indeed it took up so much space on the deck of the little yacht that it rather ruins the overall elegance. It is understandable however that, having to embark and disembark high and very high ranking passengers in all weathers, it was preferable to have on hand a more stable craft with higher sides. There were in fact various possible types of craft and Cleveley's picture allows us to establish precisely which type *Royal Caroline* carried. The boat in the painting has a squared stern and slight sheer. She seems to have been clinker built, and despite her gilded scrolled frieze on a blue ground, was neither a slim whaler nor a richly decorated ceremonial barge, not even a heavy duty longboat. The type which corresponds best to the boat in the painting seems to be a yawl, with some extra embellishments not usually found on warships. We started from an eighteenth century 27-foot yawl and added what could be inferred from Cleveley.

We have also added drawings to illustrate how such a yawl could have been rigged for sailing and how an awning or canopy could be erected aft to shelter important passengers from the elements or prying eyes. Finally there is an illustration of a slightly more ornate light craft of the barge type (see drawings E3, E8 and E9), a vessel which might have been used as an alternative for state occasions.

ARMAMENT

Royal Caroline was armed with eight 4-pounders placed on the main deck and with eight half-pounder swivels positioned along the bulwarks. In our reconstruction we have had to deduce the shape and size of the guns from a single source, the then current English Gun Establishment. These regulations were only indicative, as there were many exceptions, so we cannot claim to have reproduced perfectly the form of the barrel, the carriage or the accessories installed on board.

According to these rules, the sizes of the various parts were in ratio to the diameter of the shot, roughly speaking the diameter of the bore. This established empirically that the stoutness of the various components was in proportion to the stresses which they had to bear.

First of all, the length of the barrel had to be established. It could vary considerably, even for pieces of the same calibre, which also happens in contemporary artillery. In the eighteenth century the enormous variety which had existed in previous centuries had mostly given way to a certain rationalization. There were 'long' pieces measuring 22 or 24 times their calibre, which had a longer range and were more accurate over long distances than normal pieces. There were also short pieces measuring 15 or 18 times their calibre which had the advantage of weighing less. In the Royal Navy during this period, the most frequently used pieces were 18 or 20 calibres in length. It was common for a pair of long, small-calibre pieces called 'chasers' to be carried on the forecastle. Aft, under the stern, big ships had two or four ports through which guns taken from their normal broadside position could fire, though long pieces were more common in this position.

The thickness of the metal of the muzzle varied according to calibre and length. A barrel 24 calibres long was thicker than one of 15 which fired the same ball. The thickness also varied according to whether the barrel was made from iron or brass. It was easier to obtain a good quality cast in brass than in iron, so brass cannons were generally not as thick as iron ones, and they were safer until the art of iron smelting reached a certain quality. Brass guns were much more costly (4 to 5 times the cost of iron) and stood up to prolonged use less well because brass was corroded by the combustion gas of the powder. Midway through the eighteenth century iron smelting no longer presented insurmountable difficulties and the use of iron came therefore to predominate for large guns in the Royal Navy; we can be almost certain that the barrels of the small guns of *Royal Caroline* were brass.

Our reconstruction is based on the supposition that these guns were brass, 20 calibres in length. The diameter of the iron ball, weighing 4 pounds, was just over 3 inches (7.7cm). At the muzzle, excluding the swell, the external diameter of the barrel measured little more than 2 calibres and 3 to 3.5 at the breech. The thickness of the components of the carriage was also proportional to the bore. The thickness of the sides was one calibre for iron guns while those made of brass could be thinner. The diameters of the bolts holding the various pieces of the carriage together were one fifth of the bore. The carriage had to be high enough to align the axis of the bore with the centre of the port, at 6.5 calibres height from the deck. Generally the port measured 6.5 calibres in width by 6 in height and the distance between the centres of the ports of the same battery was 25 calibres.

These rules will give the reader some idea, but they were often ignored. One only has to think of a ship rearmed with guns other than its original armament (for instance with short 24-pound pieces instead of long 18-pounders). The ports would be smaller and the carriages lower than the regulation dimensions. Then there was the strange habit, followed by many foundries, of casting the guns with low trunnions. When trunnions were low, their axis was no longer in line with that of the bore, but about one third of the barrel section below it, so when the gun was fired a torque was created which increased the tendency of the front wheels to kick up. We do not know what advantages outweighed this and many eighteenth century writers on artillery agreed in condemning this practice. The shape of the carriage for guns with low trunnions was slightly different from the others.

MASTS AND SPARS

The proportions of the masting in relation to the hull and of all the accessories to each other were established in all navies according to tradition (in the merchant fleet in the eighteenth century tradition was the only real authority on such matters) or to rules laid down by offices or bodies appointed for the purpose. This was the Navy Board for the Royal Navy in England. The year in which *Royal Caroline* was built, 1749, came between two years in which far-reaching changes were decided, with the issue of the 1745 and 1773 Establishments. Evidence before and after these dates must be considered with some caution.

The National Maritime Museum plans give no indication for reconstructing the masting apart from the position and inclination of the masts, the number of deadeyes on the chainwales and some other scraps of information. We have, it is true, Cleveley's painting as a primary source, and we have drawn on this in many cases; nevertheless, the level of detail which it provides is insufficient. Though the eighteenth century in England is generally well covered by naval historians, deciding on the masting details of a specific ship of a given period, in this case a ship of the Sixth Rate of 1749, raises problems. David Steel's *Elements of Rigging* is certainly detailed and reliable, but not contemporary (the first edition dates from 1794). The same can be said of D'Arcy Lever. Sutherland, Falconer, Murray and Hutchinson are lacking in precise references to the specific subject.

Fortunately, James Lees's book on this particular subject was published in 1979. Mr Lees has had the opportunity of studying the incomparable collection of models belonging to the National Maritime Museum and he has evaluated them critically in the light of written sources. His work will certainly remain a classic on Royal Navy rigging during that period. It has clarified a number of doubtful points and greatly reduced the margin of error here.

Mast making. It is known that the lower masts of big ships consisted of several parts, taken from different trunks. The topmasts and yards (except the very largest yards) were shaped from a single tree-trunk. As early as the eighteenth century the scarcity of timber for shipbuilding was already being felt in Europe, particularly of curved oak for the framing of the hull and straight conifer trunks for the masts. The masts of a small ship like *Royal Caroline* could have been made in several pieces or shaped from a single trunk, which was certainly possible, given their size. On the other hand, the masts of a 36-gun frigate which Steel shows as made (in rather a complicated fashion) were not much bigger than those of *Royal Caroline*. Moreover, as *Royal Caroline* was a royal yacht, all the materials would have been of the best possible quality. As made masts were considered to be better than pole masts, we have drawn *Royal Caroline*'s main and foremast as made and left the mizzen as a pole mast. The visible difference is limited to the presence of iron hoops around the main and foremasts.

Colour of masts. The colour and general appearance of the lower masts, whether made or not, is also important. Written sources are generally unhelpful, so it is necessary to examine the models. Some of these still have their original masts, and a significant minority of these masts are painted, usually yellow ochre, mustard, cream or something between these. Since models with artifically coloured masts are a positive and unequivocal indication, the masts of *Royal Caroline* are shown painted in this book.

All masts had from the trestletrees and crosstrees up to the cap painted black. On top and topgallant masts, the black part extended under the trestletrees and crosstrees to include the hounds. Apart from the heel and head, top and topgallant masts were left their natural colour.

All masts were fitted with rope wooldings and wooden hoops. (The prevailing opinion is that these hoops were originally used to protect the rope woolding). The hoops were nailed to the masts and sometimes painted red, but more often black.

The spar plan. We have taken *Royal Caroline*'s masting as normally rigged, including staysails, but without studding sails. There is no trace of stunsail booms or irons in Cleveley's painting, and he would not have omitted them. Nevertheless, since both George II and his grandson George III were greatly interested in innovations in sailing it is not unlikely that the ship did have a complete set of studding sails, plus all the accessories, even if they were not normally used.

Royals were known in the 1600s; the first ship to hoist them on the three masts was the legendary *Sovereign of the Seas* of 1637. Nevertheless, apart from certain occasional appearances as experiments or displays of ambitious captains, royals were not used in the Royal Navy for the whole first half of the eighteenth century, so we can be certain that *Royal Caroline* did not normally carry royals, except perhaps towards the end of her career.

The bowsprit carried a jibboom and a spritsail yard, but not a sprit topmast. This characteristic feature of square rigged seventeenth century ships (its first appearance dates from around 1590) began to fall into disuse on smaller English craft around the start of the 1700s and it was gradually abolished on larger ships in the first quarter of that century.

The jibboom which replaced the sprit topmast could easily be drawn in and lashed parallel to the bowsprit, which was a great advantage in bad weather. In its normal position the boom was made fast around the bowsprit, at an angle of 45 degrees from the vertical, by an iron band. On the bowsprit there was also a vertical staff which carried the jack.

Though the spritsail became less important after the advent of jibsails, its function had been to control the trim of the ship with beam winds. With wind from aft, it was the ideal sail for keeping the bow to leeward and countering a tendency to yaw. We have included the spritsail among the ship's usual complement. It is shown reefed in Cleveley's painting.

Royal Caroline retained the mizzen yard extending forward of the mast, although this extension was without a sail. The passage to the more 'modern' shaped gaff took place on Royal Navy small craft from 1745 onwards, and from about 1780 on larger ships. The retention of the older spar was justified by the fact that the mizzen yard could be used as a spare mast or yard. Although the yard was retained, the sail was cut so that its luff could be laced to the mast.

Topmasts. At the sides of the main and foremast heads there were two cheek blocks used for ropes which will be dealt with in greater detail below. These cheek blocks were fixed to the mast by tenons which fitted into mortices cut into the head. The pins on which the sheaves turned passed through the head and kept the cheek blocks in position. The pins themselves were locked by a gib. The inside of the blocks was coppered for greater solidity.

The two sheaves let into the heel of the topmasts were used for hoisting and lowering the mast. This meant that the topmast could be hoisted into position or lowered to the deck at sea; a rope, known as the top rope, passed through the sheave and led to the capstan. In *Royal Caroline*, as was standard practice on eighteenth century ships, this device was double with the two cables crossing each other. The same system was used for the topgallant masts, for which, however, the rope was never doubled.

The manoeuvre of lowering a topmast, somewhat simplified, was as follows. The top rope was fixed to the cap of the lower mast which had two eyebolts on its lower surface for this purpose. It ran through the sheave in the topmast heel, then through a block stropped under the cap on the other side, then descended to the deck and was taken to the capstan, passing through a sheave hole in the bitts. The topsail yard was lowered to the top. The topmast shrouds and backstays were slackened and the lower yard truss ropes eased at the same time and the yard hauled forward so that the topmast could pass between the yard and the lower mast. Tackles were fixed to the backstays and stays to keep them taut so as to hold the mast vertical as it was descending, because neither the shrouds nor the stays could have supported it during the manoeuvre. The top rope was then hauled taut by the capstan, the mast was raised a fraction and the fid, which kept the mast heel in position above the trestletrees, could be pulled out (or knocked out) of its housing. The top rope was gradually slackened, and the mast passed down through the round hole in the cap until it reached the desired position where it was lashed to the lower mast. The topmast shrouds were tied in bunches above the top so that they offered less resistance to the wind, and the topsail yard lashed to the chainplates of the topmast shrouds, with the tie and the braces taut for greater security. In some situations it was preferable to leave the topsail yard on its mast rather than lowering it to the top as described. When the topmast was lashed to the lower mast in the position described above, the sail could always be used, reefed to the maximum.

TOPS, TRESTLETREES AND CAPS

The *Royal Caroline* tops were built according to the 1745 Establishments, which differ very little from those of the beginning or the end of the century. The platform was light, but strong, built of 2-inch fir planks. The planking was laid in the traditional way, which can be seen in drawings G1–G3, and nailed where they crossed. In the Royal Navy elm wood was used for the rim reinforcement and the battens. These reinforcing pieces were not nailed but fixed to the platform with treenails. In the Royal Navy the planks were laid alongside each other without any spaces between and known as 'closed tops', as opposed to practice in the merchant fleet, in which gaps were left between the planks; this was also usual in other navies.

The top platform was built separately and then, fitted with all its reinforcements, hoisted to the mast head using a special rope and fixed to the trestletrees and crosstrees using bolts locked with gibs placed below the trestletrees and crosstrees. Six bolts (three for each side) on each of the crosstrees and four on each trestletree were, we feel, the right number for *Royal Caroline*. The mizzen top probably required fewer bolts, (four and three respectively). The top could then be repaired without having to dismantle the loadbearing structure of the crosstrees and trestletrees.

The light aft parapet of the tops generally consisted of 2- to 3-inch section wooden stanchions turned in various ways and joined to a rail at the top. On small ships the stanchions were often in iron, and this is what we have chosen for the yacht. In the period in which *Royal Caroline* was extant the space between the stanchions was mostly left open or filled with rope netting. Many models dating from the first half of the century have a canvas covering, sometimes red and decorated with coats of arms, a gold border or other ornamentation. A painting of *Royal Caroline* at the time of the 1761 crossing shows a covering of this kind, but this was a gala occasion and we believe that this type of covering was only used on such occasions and removed as soon as possible in view of its unfavourable effect on the ship's trim.

The colour of the top is not as simple as it may seem. Neither contemporary nor modern written evidence contains details of this kind. The evidence from models is that the tops of English eighteenth century ships were generally painted black, though there are exceptions. In the absence of any indications to the contrary, it can be assumed that *Royal Caroline*'s tops were painted the usual black.

The construction of the topmast trestletrees and crosstrees is clear from drawing G6. This light structure served mainly as a base for the topgallant mast

shrouds and a housing for the heel of these masts. The first ships we know of which had trestletrees and crosstrees without the earlier topmast tops were Dutch, dating from the early seventeenth century.

It is worthwhile devoting a few words to caps (drawing G7). These important masting elements were made of elm wood in English ships. The wood was taken from that part of the trunk close to the roots where the grain was particularly contorted so that a block of it did not easily split lengthwise. When a big enough piece could not be found, the cap was made in two pieces. The two halves were dovetailed together lengthwise, at least according to Steel. Whether the cap was made in one piece or in two, strong reinforcing bolts were run through it crosswise and clinched over roves to prevent it from breaking under strain. There were three bolts at either end of the cap and two in the centre. The round hole to take the topmast had a protective leather lining nailed to the upper and lower faces of the cap.

The topmast caps were constructed using the same principles (but always from a single block of elm). Again according to Steel, there were two transverse reinforcing bolts at each end and one in the middle.

STANDING RIGGING

The complexity of the rigging on three-masted, square rigged ships arose mainly from the limitations of the available materials. All materials were vegetable in origin: wood for the masts and spars, hemp for ropes, hemp again for the sails, tar to impregnate the ropes, wood again for the blocks and so on. The importance of the cordage is obvious at first sight.

Ropemaking. Ropes in pre-industrial times were valued and widely used, and their manufacture and preservation were the object of painstaking attention. The ropemaker's craft was noteworthy for its costly equipment by pre-industrial standards, and its high degree of precision.

The ropes used on European ships during the eighteenth century consisted almost exclusively of hemp fibre. Hemp ropes deteriorated rapidly with alternating moisture and dryness. For standing rigging, they were impregnated with tar to preserve them, which also made the rope less flexible and elastic; tarred ropes were slightly less strong than the white rope used for running rigging, but they lasted much longer. The tar used in the time of *Royal Caroline* was vegetable tar made from the distillation of coniferous wood, of an oily consistency and brown in colour. It was quite different from the black, sticky tar we know today, which is a by-product of the distillation of mineral oil. This brown colour immediately distinguished the standing rigging of an old ship, lanyards and serving included, from the running rigging.

Serving was one of the most frequently used methods for protecting the rigging from rubbing against the masts or the other ropes. Serving a cable meant 'bandaging' it with pieces of old sails (a process known as 'parcelling') and then binding twine tightly round it in the opposite direction using a special tool. The big cables of standing rigging were also 'wormed', which meant a finer rope about one tenth of the main cable diameter was spirally wound in the grooves between its individual strands to protect them from the elements. A stay, then, could be wormed and served for most of its length.

The running rigging had to remain flexible and so was not tarred, nor served nor wormed. It retained its yellowish hemp colour, which became greyish with the passage of time.

It is perhaps appropriate to proceed in the same order in which the rigging was fitted to the masts in the dockyard. The riggers always started from the bowsprit and followed the same sequence which was dictated by the logic of their work.

Bowsprit. The gammoning was the first piece of rigging to be set up and consisted of running from nine to eleven turns of rope round the mast and through an oblong hole in the stem. The *Royal Caroline* gammoning was 4cm in diameter and arranged as illustrated in drawing H24. The outer extremity of the bowsprit was weighted down while the gammoning was being laid (usually a tackle was attached to the bottom of a heavily ballasted boat and tightened). The gammoning itself was laboriously set up by tackles fastened to the capstan.

Then came the bobstay collars (in the case of *Royal Caroline* one only) and the collars of the bowsprit shrouds. These were of cable-laid rope and were wormed and served. The bobstay passed through a hole in the stem. It was double and wormed and served along its entire length. The forward end carried a heart block which was paired with that on the collar mounted on the mast. The bowsprit shrouds were set up by deadeyes. The inner end of the shroud, which was of double, wormed and served, cable-laid rope, was hooked to an eyebolt in the bows. Them the big collar of the forestay was fitted to the bowsprit, also double and wormed and served along its entire length.

At this point the (double) collar of the mainstay was led through the hole in the stem below the bowsprit and spliced. Then the riggers moved on to the other masts.

The shrouds. First the riggers placed a length of rope spliced to form a ring, called a grommet, at the base of the main, mizzen and foremast heads. This served as a buffer for the standing rigging and avoided direct contact with the wood. Then came the pendants of tackles made of cable-laid rope the same diameter as the shrouds and served and wormed along their entire length. The heavy blocks which formed the runners of the tackles were only attached to the pendants when this equipment was required. Then the shrouds were fitted, in pairs, starting from the forward ones; it was English practice always to begin each pair from the starboard side.

The shrouds of English warships, according to Steel, were cable laid, that is left-handed, and of four strands. There was a fifth strand called a 'heart' in the middle of the four strands which gave greater firmness to the rope. When shrouds were prepared they were first of all stretched by a capstan until the heart broke. The operation was performed repeatedly until the cable was well stretched along its entire length and it was then left under tension for a certain period of time. Then the shrouds were wormed and served at the bight and down to just below the futtock stave. The part protected in this way was about a quarter of the total length of the shroud. The first forward shroud was completely wormed and served to protect it from the sail, the yard and the running rigging chafing against it. The bights were closed by a seizing. The first seizing was put just under the bolster (the term for the rounded softwood piece placed above the trestletrees which protected the shrouds from being rubbed). The other seizings were arranged above, one after the other in such a way that they did not rub against each other. At this point the deadeyes were turned into the shrouds. Experience had shown that the best way to attach the cable to the deadeye for maximum duration and minimum wear was, for a left-handed cable, to pass the end of the shroud round the deadeye from left to right, looking from inboard, cross the main part of the shroud inboard and seize it on the left of the main part of the shroud. The lanyard was then passed from the inside to the outside through the first hole in the upper deadeye at the side of the main part of the shroud. The end of the lanyard had a stopper knot which locked it into the hole of the deadeye. The other end, once the shroud was tightened, was passed several times around the shroud and finally seized to it. The diameter of the lanyard was half that of the shroud.

The shrouds were provisionally set up using a tackle made with double or treble blocks (cables of that thickness could not be hauled taut by hand). The simplest arrangement was this: the upper block of the tackle was seized to the shroud itself a little way above the deadeye. The lower block was seized to the lanyard. Hauling the tackle taut set up the shroud. There were more elaborate systems for the shrouds of larger ships, consisting of a double tackle. When the shroud was new the distance between the deadeyes had to be, in theory, twice the deadeye diameter. The deadeyes tended to end up touching each other as the shroud stretched with use; when this happened the crew had to take steps to shorten the cables.

The stays. The riggers then hoisted the stay bight between the trestletrees and above the mast head and then they lowered and arranged it above the shrouds. Then they proceeded to set up the lanyard of the stay with the help of a tackle, as for the shrouds. The stay was entirely wormed and served to below the mouse (a knob of spun yarn which engaged in the eye of the stay and prevented the bight from becoming too tight around the mast). A bight formed in this manner offered far greater resistance to strain than the earlier system of a simple eye splice around the mast. The mouse, according to Steel, had to be three times the diameter of the stay itself.

The main and foremasts, in addition to the topmasts, were fitted with preventer stays on warships in case the stays were shot away in battle. Their introduction in the early 1700s was gradual. *Royal Caroline* most probably did not have preventer stays since Cleveley has not shown them and there are other examples of small ships dating from the mid-century which were not fitted with them.

Catharpins. Next the riggers fitted the shrouds with a futtock stave below the trestletrees at the same distance from them as the cap was above them. The catharpins were lashed to the shrouds and to the futtock stave and bowsed in the shrouds, to tighten them. The futtock staves spread the strain of the topmast shrouds on the lower ones so that the topmast shrouds could be evenly hauled taut. They were each formed of a piece of thick cable-laid rope which was wormed, served and tarred so that it stayed stiff.

In addition to these upper catharpins, lower catharpins were also commonly fitted. They were placed halfway along the shrouds and were used to tighten them quickly when they were too slack or when the mast needed more support in bad weather. Note that on similar occasions the runners of tackles and even the toprope were rigged. These ropes were hauled taut on the windward side to support the shrouds. The lower catharpins fell into disuse as standing rigging during the first decades of the eighteenth century, but they were rigged when required right into the nineteenth century. One simple method of rigging these catharpins consisted of running a rope alternately from one side to another through a series of blocks seized to the shrouds.

Rigging the topmasts. It was only at this point that the riggers hoisted the tops above the masthead in a rather spectacular operation (the top of a big ship weighed a ton or more) and fixed them in position using bolts running through the trestletrees and crosstrees. Then the topmasts were hoisted by means of a rope rigged more or less like a temporary toprope (the actual toprope could not be rigged as the cap was not yet in position). When the head of the topmast came level with the platform of the top, the riggers passed it through the round hole of the lower mast cap which they had previously positioned. The cap was provisionally lashed to the topmast. Raising the topmast further pulled the cap along until it reached the right level in relation to the lower masthead; the cap could then be fitted to the masthead and untied from the topmast. A good many vigorous blows from a mallet were needed to lock the square tenon into the mortice cut into the lower face of the cap because very little play could be allowed. At this point the riggers fitted the trestletrees and crosstrees to the topmast head. To do this the fully assembled trestletrees and crosstrees were hoisted and placed on the cap of the lower mast so that the topmast, raised a little, fitted into its position in the frame formed by the trestletrees and crosstrees. Then the standing rigging was fitted to the topmast head and finally its cap.

For the topmasts the riggers followed the same assembly sequence as for the lower masts: first a protective grommet was fitted around the masthead, then the burton pendants (which were similar in function to the pendants of tackles for the lower masts), then the shrouds, the backstays and finally the stays. At this point the real toprope was rigged and the fully fitted topmast was hoisted into place and stopped with the fid which ran athwartships through the heel and locked onto the trestletrees. Next came the job of setting up the topmast shrouds and then the stays, as for the lower masts. The riggers passed the topmast deadeye plates into the holes prepared in the topmast rim, hooked the futtock shrouds onto the deadeye plates, passed them around the futtock stave and seized them onto the lower shrouds. The shrouds were then set up by means of a tackle which was hooked to the burton pendants (or on the mizzen, to a strop fitted to the mast head) and worked as for the lower masts both on the shroud and its lanyard. The topmast shrouds had a futtock stave to anchor the topgallant shrouds but no catharpins.

Backstays. The top- and topgallant masts were held laterally by backstays and topgallant backstays as well as shrouds; these also transferred the strain directly to the hull. Apart from standing backstays set up by deadeyes like the shrouds, one or two running backstays could be fitted as required. These were ropes, of the same diameter as their respective shroud, to which was spliced a block forming a tackle. The running backstays thus could be hove taut or slackened much more easily than with a pair of deadeyes and permitted the mast to be supported appropriately in all situations by changing their position. There were various eyebolts available on the chainwales and inboard. At the time of *Royal Caroline*, running backstays were used only for the main and fore masts, and they were officially adopted at the mizzen only after 1770. For ships of *Royal Caroline*'s size they consisted of a 1-inch rope hove taut by a tackle formed with two single 5-inch blocks.

Royal Caroline's main and fore standing backstays were set up using deadeyes, those of the mizzen using hearts and the topgallant backstays, thimbles. The fore topgallant backstays, with their thimbles, were set up on the same chains which held the topmast backstay deadeyes.

Rigging the topgallants. The same sequence used for the topmasts was followed in setting up the topgallant masts. The topgallant shrouds passed through the holes made in the ends of the crosstrees and were lashed onto the futtock stave of the topmast shrouds. At the time of *Royal Caroline* an eye splice with a thimble was made at the end of the fore, main and mizzen topgallant shrouds, though deadeyes had remained in use up to 1719; when shrouds were equipped with chainplates running through the crosstrees, like the topmast shrouds. When the use of royals became general in a later period, and the topgallant shrouds therefore had to withstand greater strain, the shrouds ran inside the futtock stave, down along the topmast shrouds, and were set up with thimbles to the chainplates of the topmast shrouds themselves. This gave a more elastic support because the rope was much longer and the topmast shrouds were not strained at the futtock stave, which did not provide a rigid enough support.

Methods of setting up stays. The lower fore, main and mizzen stays can clearly be seen in the rigging plan but the others need clarification. The fore topmast stay (a four-strand, cable-laid rope 4cm in diameter) ran through a block stropped to the bowsprit and was hove taut by a tackle hooked to an eyebolt on the starboard knighthead.

The main topmast stay ran through a block stropped to the foremast head. From here it ran between the trestletrees aft of the mast and down along the mast and was hove taut on the deck by a tackle consisting of a long-tackle block and a single one. The long-tackle block was 40.4cm long (overall) and the single one was half this. The runners of the tackles were 2cm diameter ropes.

The mizzen topmast stay was set up by two deadeyes on the mainmast below the start of the cheeks. The diameter of the deadeyes was the same as those of the mizzen topmast shrouds (12.7cm). The collar, completely served, was 2cm, and the runner 1cm.

The foretopgallant stay ran through the central sheave of the treble block stropped at the end of the jibboom and was set up by means of a pair of thimbles on the knighthead below the fore topmast stay. The main topgallant stay ran through a block stropped to the fore topmast head and was led to the top. The mizzen topgallant stay ran through a block fixed to an eyebolt on the aft face of the main cap and was lashed to the mainstay collar.

THE SAILS

Information available on the art of sailmaking in the Royal Navy is scarce, as the first written source dates from 1794 (Steel). However, there are the models, although the oldest English model with original sails is the *Tartar*, a 20-gun ship dating from 1734. Therefore, much of what follows, relating to a ship of about 1750, is the result of careful deduction.

Sailmaking. The strips of cloth used to make sails in the Royal Navy were 24, 25, 26 or 30 inches wide in the periods that are documented. At the time of *Royal Caroline* the 24-inch width was normally used for all sails. The Royal Navy used hemp exclusively, but of different thicknesses depending on whether it was for courses or topsails. In the Mediterranean a lighter fabric mixture of hemp and cotton was in use during the eighteenth and nineteenth centuries with pure hemp cloth used to reinforce the more exposed points. In making the sails the strips of cloth were overlapped and double stitched. The overlap was 1½ inches for the courses and topsails on ships of more than 50 guns, 1¼ inches for the same sails on smaller ships and 1 inch for all other sails (Steel). The stitching, done in the best quality twine, had to be 108 stitches to the yard (91cm) so each stitch must have been 8 to 9mm at the most.

A brief review of the relevant terminology will be a help in understanding the rest of this section. Square sails are described as having a head (the top side which is attached to the yard), a leech on either side and a foot (or bottom edge) which can have a roach (a hollow foot). In the merchant navy the top- and topgallant sails always had a roach to stop them from chafing against the stays, but in the Royal Navy, the wear was considered preferable to losing the wind which escaped from the hollow foot. So their sails were cut straight even though paintings, prints, etc, make them look curved when full of wind. The foot of the sail was lined with leather to stop it from wearing.

The sail was folded over and stitched down (or 'tabled') right round the edge. Then a stout rope called a bolt rope was stitched all round the edge and this directly took the strain at the points where the rigging was made fast to the sail. The stitching ran through the bolt rope and the tabling of the sail. At certain points on the bolt rope, cringles were worked for attaching rigging. These were formed by strands of rope spliced on to it. Leeches and other points subject to particular wear had reinforcing strips (such as mast cloths, reef bands, leech linings and foot linings) stitched to them.

The triangular staysails (or the jibsail) had an edge for attaching to the stay, or staysail stay, called a stay, a leech (after edge) and a foot. Its corners were termed peak (the top one), tack (the forward one) and clue (where the sheet was fastened). In the Royal Navy during the time of *Royal Caroline* the stitching was done in the following order: the canvas was folded over at the edge to form the tabling, always on the aft side of square sails. The depth of the tabling ranged from 6 inches for a course to 2 for a topgallant sail. The reef bands were sewn on the fore side of the sail and were one-third of a cloth wide for courses and half a cloth for topsails. The leech linings were also sewn onto the fore side of the sail above the reef bands. The mast cloths of the topsails were stitched to the aft side of the sail, the only exception among the reinforcements. The fore and aft sails had the linings and tabling on the port side. The triangular staysails had no lining on the tabling but had a bolt rope. The mizzen sail had the tabling on the port side like all fore and aft sails and a lining on the forward edge where (in the period of *Royal Caroline*) holes were made for the luff lacing to pass through and round the mast.

Rigging the sails. Square sails were attached to the yards by means of robands which, at the time of *Royal Caroline*, were simply passed round the yard and through the roband holes twice and tied with a reef knot above the yard. In more recent times these robands were tied in much more complicated knots. There were two roband holes for each cloth. The reef points passed through their holes (two per cloth) and were made fast by one knot on the fore and another on the aft side of the sail. The overall length of the reef points was roughly twice the circumference of the yard on the first reef band (the top one). The reef points of the other reef bands were proportionately longer since the cloth to be reefed around the yard was bulkier. Two-thirds of the reef point length hung on the after side of the sail and one-third on the forward one. This is because the men who were reefing the sails, lying with their chests on the yard, once they had gathered in the sail, knotted the reef points on the forward side of the yard. The number of reef bands has varied through history. Up to 1680, the surface of the courses was reduced using bonnets – strips of cloth laced to the foot of the sail.

About this time, bonnets stopped being used and a reef band was introduced on fore and main courses (reef bands were introduced on topsails some 20 to 30 years earlier). The second reef band was introduced much later, around 1840 (according to Lees). This rule of only one reef band on courses and three to four on topsails evidently had many exceptions since Cleveley distinctly illustrates two reef bands on *Royal Caroline*'s courses, and we have respected this. The ship is portrayed sailing under a fresh breeze with one reef taken in on the main and mizzen topsails and two on the fore. With the reefs taken, this gives a total of three reef bands on the main and fore topsails and two on the mizzen. This agrees with the chronology given by Lees for the introduction of the third reef band on the main and fore courses and the second on the mizzen in 1710. Reef point and roband holes pierced in the canvas were reinforced by grommets or rope yarn stitched around them.

Two distinct types of gaskets, known as sea and harbour, were used to hold the sails to the yard when furled. At sea, when the sail was furled using leechlines, buntlines and so on, a variable number of ropes was wound round the yard and the sail from the centre to the yard arm. There were eight of these gaskets on large ships and at least four on small ones, two per side. One end was spliced around the yard and the other was loose. When the gasket was not in use, it was rolled up and placed on the yard.

Harbour gaskets were used in port and there were from eight to twelve of them. They consisted of short lengths of braided cord spliced on top of the

yard. They passed once round the sail and yard and were tied to themselves on the other side. In port also a bunt gasket was used. This was a triangle of strong canvas or rope netting, one side of which was fixed to the yard between the strops of the quarter blocks through which the topsail sheets rove. The apex of the triangle carried two ropes for hauling the bunt gasket upwards from the top to carry the central, bulkier part of the sail above the yard. We do not know if the bunt gasket was in use as early as 1750. It must be remembered that during the eighteenth century and before, sails were attached directly to the yards because jackstays were not introduced in England until 1811. Here too we believe that this official date of introduction had been preceded by use in the merchant navy anyway. It often happened that innovations became established by their use on merchantmen, whose captains and owners had much greater freedom to please themselves. So before 1811, sails hung below the yards and not in front of them as after the introduction of jackstays. When a sail was furled or reefed, the canvas ended up beneath the yard. The position of buntlines, leechlines and cluelines, in particular, was such that the canvas was evenly distributed along the yard and not bunched centrally. So, an eighteenth-century ship with sails furled looked different from a nineteenth century one which had the sails gathered on top of the yard with the bulk placed centrally where the bunt gasket hung.

These matters are covered in much greater depth in *Seamanship in the Age of Sail* by Harland and Myers. We mention them to illustrate how minor changes in rigging are not without consequences. Moving the position of the leechline, buntline and clueline blocks on the yards involved a different way of furling the sail and could only occur by handling the sail differently when furled.

RUNNING RIGGING TO THE YARDS

The order in which the running rigging was fitted to the yards was not dictated by the assembly requirements, as in standing rigging. The yards were fitted as required ashore and then taken on board and hoisted into position.

The order of rigging the lower yards. First the stirrups and footropes were fitted. The stirrups were 3 feet long and attached to the yard by being wound round it three times and nailed down using short, flat-headed nails. The part that was nailed down was first unlaid and the loose strands braided together to make the stirrups stronger.

The yard arm tackles came next and consisted of a pendant spliced to the yard arm which carried a long-tackle block, which formed a tackle with a hooked block. This tackle was used for hoisting heavy weights such as boats and the like. Then the brace pendants with their blocks were fitted. The lower yards on warships were fitted with preventer braces when a battle was expected. These ran forward, in the opposite direction to the braces whose job they took over if they were sheared; obviously the preventer braces are not shown in our rigging plan. The topsail sheet stoppers were spliced onto the yard arm, immediately next to the brace pendants. They consisted of a short length of rather stout rope which was tied to the topsail clue before a battle. Its purpose was to hold the clue should the sheet break. Next came the topsail sheet blocks whose strops also carried blocks for the lower lifts. The special shape of these sheet blocks (shoulder blocks) prevented the topsail sheet from jamming between the yard and the block when under strain. The big jeer blocks were next. The lower and topsail yard jeers and ties were among the rigging items most subject to changes in lead. At the time of the *Royal Caroline* the jeers of the main and fore yards were rigged with two single blocks on the yard and two double blocks stropped to the masthead above the shrouds (Lees). Around 1773, a type of 'jeer-tie', consisting of a single block stropped to the yard and two single blocks stropped to the mast, was introduced for the lower yards of small ships. The runner, consisting of a single rope, passed through the block stropped to the yard, then from either side, through the blocks stropped to the mast and ran down to the deck. A double block was spliced at each end of the jeer and formed a tackle with a treble block hooked to an eyebolt on the deck. Steel quotes this device for 24-gun and smaller ships in 1794, but according to Cleveley, *Royal Caroline* was so fitted. The painting shows a large single block stropped to the centre of the main and fore yards. The innovation (if it can be called this because, from the theoretical point of view, it was reverting to ancient usage) must have occurred, in practice, a good deal earlier than 1773.

At this time, ships, whether large or small, did not have slings for the lower yards; these came into use in 1773. So the weight of the yard and sail was borne constantly by the jeers or ties.

Then the quarter blocks for the topsail sheets were fixed to the yard not far from the centre and the other blocks for the buntlines and leechlines. Then came the truss, which must have been the traditional type with parrels, according to Lees who states that truss pendants (termed 'English' by Stratico and 'rope trusses' by Roeding) were introduced around 1760. So we have reproduced parrels for the lower yards even if we have some doubts as to whether the new, much simpler type was not already in use by 1750. We have noted that *Royal Caroline* often had some rigging features which deviated from the Establishments. Parrels were useful when it was the practice to lower the yards to the gunwales to furl the sail. This practice had been abandoned by the Royal Navy perhaps before the beginning of the eighteenth century, therefore the old parrel trusses were of little use to the lower yards.

The crossjack. This mizzen yard had some peculiarities which need to be explained. First, it did not have jeers, but a sling which was unlike those rigged on the other lower yards after 1773. Steel gives 2.8cm as the diameter of a sling for a ship of *Royal Caroline*'s rate. The sling ran through a 28cm block which was stropped to the crossjack. The lead of the braces was also unusual. They were led forward rather than aft like the rest and crossed as well, *ie* each taken to the opposite side of the ship. This was to permit greater force to be exerted on the yard when it had to be braced to the maximum. Finally the lifts of the crossjack were fitted with two single blocks stropped to the cap while long-tackle blocks were used for the main and fore yards.

Rigging the topmast yards. The footropes came first, followed by the braces, then the lifts, the ties, the truss and the other minor ropes. Then came the reef tackles which will be mentioned in the section dealing with running rigging to the sails. Here an important point must be made about the lifts. Up to 1790 the topsail lifts were used as topgallant sheets. When the topgallant sail was furled, the topsail lifts started from the cap, ran to the block stropped to the topsail yardarm, from here to a block attached by a long strop to the mast head, and then to the deck (see drawing H16). This is precisely the lead which Cleveley shows in his painting, where the ship's topgallants have been taken in. When these were set, the lifts were untied from the pendant on the cap and tied to the clues of the sail.

A lot could be said on the subject of the topsail ties whose lead is shown in drawing H14, since the riggers gave rein to their imagination with this rope. We shall not go into the successive variations over time, even for the Royal Navy alone, but just clarify why its rigging was so complicated. Before the arrangement shown in H14 was adopted, there were single ties on the main and foremast and they went from the mast head, through a single block stropped to the yard, back up again to a second block stropped to the mast head and down

to the deck, either to starboard or port (normally the foremast to port and the main to starboard). This had the disadvantage that in 50 per cent of the cases, one had to haul from the leeward side with consequent danger to the topmast. Then someone thought of doubling the rope as illustrated, so that it could always be hauled from the weather side. This type of double tie could still function even if one of the two was damaged in battle or manoeuvring in bad weather. The English adopted it in 1685. Its adoption by the Continental navies in the middle of the following century proved that it was an excellent device. The mizzen topsail tie kept its simpler older lead, perhaps because this sail was never used in bad weather.

The mizzen topsail and topgallant yard braces were led aft to two pairs of blocks or thimbles stropped to the end of the mizzen yard and from here to the deck. This strange lead remained in use up to the end of the eighteenth century, after which the braces were led forward like those of the crossjack, to the mainmast. On Continental ships (Dutch and French in particular) the solution of leading the braces of the mizzen topsail and topgallant yards to the mainmast was adopted from the early decades of the eighteenth century. The mizzen yard rigging is naturally a feature of this which for centuries, was the only fore and aft sail on three-masted ships.

Rigging to the topgallant yards was much simpler. The tie was single and ran through a sheave in the mast and a halyard was seized to the other end, the lower block of the tackle being seized to the lower top. The lifts were single too and, from the yard arm, went to a thimble on a short pendant on the head of the mast and were hove taut on the chainplates of the topmast shrouds. In the time of *Royal Caroline* neither buntlines nor leechlines were used on topgallant sails. The lead of the bowlines is clearly visible on the rigging plans.

RUNNING RIGGING TO THE SAILS

The main ropes which were made fast to the sails generally had simple leads which are evident from the plans. Others need some explanation. The foresail tacks, for example, in this period, led to the bumkins where a block was stropped and returned inboard to be made fast to a bitt or timber head. The tacks were not crossed as they had been before the introduction of bumkins (between 1710 and 1745, for the Royal Navy, starting with small craft, according to Lees). The tacks were subject to considerable stress and were therefore made of very thick, cable-laid rope. For *Royal Caroline* they measured 4.4cm in diameter 'at the clue'; the rope was tapered to half its diameter at the other end so that it could be handled more easily and made fast quickly as suited various trims. This treatment of the tacks is an example of the great attention given to cordage in those days. Looked at objectively, it must have been efficient because it was used in many navies (Aubin quotes 'couets a queue de rat' for the French and Dutch navies in 1701, but the oldest reference is from the Venetian navy in the early fifteenth century – 'contraschota affusada').

The course buntlines had a curious lead. The foremast lines were made fast abaft the mast but the mainmast lines went forward to the belaying pins on the forecastle rail. They were fitted with a shoe block which gave the rope a mechanical advantage and balanced the tension between the two buntline legs so that the sail was evenly furled. These small details demonstrate how the rigging of a sailing ship, after centuries of refinement, had become a complex system upon which it was difficult to improve, at least for pre-industrial technology. Imagine the crew furling a course at night with poor visibility. If each seaman hauled on the buntlines as he thought fit, the sail would be irregularly furled and the topmen would have a more difficult job. Rigging the buntlines as we have described ensured that the tension on the buntline legs was automatically balanced. The lead of the leechlines was even more curious in the Royal Navy (see drawing H18). James Lees corroborates this, as does Cleveley in his painting. In other navies the lead was similar to that of the buntlines with a lesser display of originality.

Rigging to the topsails. Two sheaves were provided in the fore and main bitts (one per side) for the topsail sheets. The bitts had another sheave on each side, to be used when required for the top rope. The two sheaves on the fore bitts were normally used for the jib and topmast staysail halyards. When the top rope had to be rigged, these two ropes were unrigged.

The topsail leechlines led from a point located among the cringles for the bowline bridles and the last reef band. They were led to a block stropped to the collar of the topsail ties, then through the inner sheave of a double block stropped under the trestletrees and from there to the deck. Lees mentions that there was an intervening passage after 1745, through another block on the yard, but Cleveley shows it in its simpler form on *Royal Caroline*, leading directly from the foot of the sail to the collar of the tie.

The other sheave of the double block stropped under the trestletrees was used for the topsail buntlines which led there directly from the foot of the sail and from there to the deck. This buntline and leechline lead was identical for the three topsails, but Lees rightly notes that the mizzen topsail was rigged as a topgallant sail when there was none at mizzen. In this case the mizzen topsail carried neither buntlines nor leechlines. In this particular period, not all ships were fitted with a mizzen topgallant sail. Their general use can be dated with certainty only after 1760. Only some models with original masting dating from 1740 to 1750 have it. Cleveley shows *Royal Caroline* with a mizzen topgallant mast in proportion to the fore and main topgallant masts, therefore we believe that she had this sail as early as 1750.

There is little to be added with regard to the topgallant sails since the sheets were dealt with along with the topmast lifts and the lead of the bowlines is clear from the rigging plan.

Staysails. These sails were most probably a northern invention, perhaps from the Netherlands or Friesland where, in the late sixteenth century, small fore and aft rigged craft were found fitted with a staysail which we would call a jib today. It was not until 1650 to 1660 that staysails were found on big three-masted ships and from then onwards they played an increasingly important role. The official date of their introduction into the Royal Navy was 1660. To these were added the jib in 1705 and the mizzen top and topgallant staysails in 1709, the fore topmast staysail in 1773 (carried on the forestay), the flying jib in 1794, and so forth. For a certain length of time a middle staysail was carried on a staysail stay which finished in a collar which ran along the fore topmast. The above dates are when a given item of rigging was officially recognised, after which the dockyards made the additions to the complements of sails, blocks etc. We can be sure that, unofficially, many ships were already carrying staysails a good many years earlier. The sails were put together on board ship using the good parts of worn sails. The captains of frigates and sloops had a reputation for spreading the maximum amount of canvas, since they were young bloods who often had the chance of sailing far from the watchful eyes of their conservative superiors.

Staysails were originally triangular in shape but after 1760 many of them became trapezoidal, and greatly increased their area (they then returned to the triangular shape around 1800). The sails included in *Royal Caroline*'s rigging plan are all triangular and they are: main topmast staysail, main topgallant staysail, a mizzen staysail and a mizzen topmast staysail, a fore topmast staysail and a jib. We have not included a main staysail, with which *Royal Caroline* was

almost certainly equipped, as it was used only in extreme weather conditions. Staysails and jibs were attached to ropes which, according to tradition or necessity, could be stays, false stays, preventer stays or staysail stays. The function of stays and preventer stays is explained above. A false stay was a stout rope seized to the stay a little below the collar and running parallel to it, set up by deadeyes placed a little below the stay heart or deadeye. A false stay was used to carry a sail. This device was used when there were blocks for other ropes on the stay and so the sail could not run along it. The staysail stay was part of the running rigging and was hove taut between two points with the sole purpose of carrying a staysail rather than to support the mast. The lighter, fair-weather jibs sometimes were not hoisted either on staysail stays or on stays but set flying.

Not all staysails were attached in the same way. At the time in question iron hanks were used, one quarter more in diameter than the stay or staysail stay on which they had to run. Alternatively, a light rope was wound round the stay in the contrary direction to its lay and through holes in the sail. According to Lees this rope attachment was in common use for all staysails before 1745 and continued to be used for the jib and the flying jib after that date. A sail attached by a rope wound like this meant that the sail could be removed and stowed without unrigging the staysail stay to which it was attached. With hanks, however, the furled sail remained attached to its stay unless it was unrigged. Logically then, a system whereby the sail could be easily removed was preferred for the fore staysails and jibs. But in this, too, *Royal Caroline* differed from the norm; Cleveley's painting clearly shows the jib attached by hanks.

The fore topmast staysail was hoisted on its staysail stay, which ran parallel to the topmast stay. The halyard was single on small ships and was seized to the peak of the sail and rove through the lower port sheave of the cheek block at the fore topmast head and then ran down to the deck. The tack consisted of a simple rope lashed to the staysail stay collar on the bowsprit. This arrangement is very much simpler than that which Lees indicates as appropriate for post-1745, which also included a fore topmast preventer stay.

The jib rigging was more complicated. The painting shows that *Royal Caroline* had a staysail stay for this sail (which was sometimes set flying). This staysail stay was attached to the traveller at the lower end. This was a large iron ring which could be moved along the jibboom by means of two ropes known as the inhauler and the outhauler. The upper end of the staysail stay rove through the upper starboard sheave of the cheek block at the fore topmast head and ran down to the chains of the starboard backstay where it was simply tied. The single halyard rove through the lower sheave of the same cheek block and was made fast to the fore bitts.

This sail was most useful in many situations. The possibility of shifting the tack along the jibboom and as a result, the position of the sail on the fore and aft plan of the ship meant that the trim of the sails could be finely adjusted much more easily than was possible by setting or reefing other sails. Before the introduction of the jib, this function was partly fulfilled by the spritsail whose suspension point originally could be moved along the bowsprit. But the jib was also an excellent sail for sailing close to the wind and, with the wind abaft, it was greatly prized for its property of raising the bows. On this point it must be noted that *Royal Caroline*'s jib is shown by Cleveley with a reef band, which was rather rare on a three-masted ship in 1750. We know of examples of late eighteenth century jibs which could be reefed (Steel mentions some, one of which was on a sloop, the smallest three-masted ship). Usually staysails with reef bands were only seen on small merchantmen.

The main topmast staysail was carried by the preventer stay. Its single halyard passed through the top starboard sheave on the topmast head and from there down to the deck. The topgallant staysail was carried on the topgallant stay. A sheave was made for its halyard in the topgallant mast immediately above the hounds. From there the halyard was led to the main top.

The mizzen stay carried the mizzen staysail and particular steps were taken to prevent it from interfering with the mizzen yard, as long as it retained its entire length. This sail was used particularly for lying-to in bad weather. The halyard was double and ran from the mast head to the block seized to the peak of the sail, then back to a block stropped to the port crosstrees and from there to the semicircular pin rack on the mizzen mast. The mizzen topmast staysail was carried by the stay. The single halyard rove through a block stropped to the mizzen topmast head or to the stay collar on the starboard side and from there to the deck.

BELAYING

Rigging arrangements on deck immediately suggest belaying pins, an accessory which is commonly, but erroneously, believed to have been present on ships of all ages. They were first used in the early seventeenth century by the Dutch navy. There is a Flemish galleon dating from 1593 in the Naval Museum of Madrid which has a few belaying pins, but it is not certain that they are original. These are the earliest known dates for belaying pins as a method for fastening rigging. They were introduced in the Royal Navy more than a century later. Lees tells us that belaying pins began to be positioned on pin racks seized to the shrouds of small ships around 1745. It is possible that their use in the merchant navy is of an earlier date. Pin racks consisting of a cross piece between the bitts were only found on English ships at the start of the nineteenth century.

Fortunately Cleveley gives a precise idea because he shows that the shrouds of all three masts carried a pin rack and the rigging trucks – which conveyed the ropes coming down from the masts parallel to the shrouds so as not to tangle with them and catch less wind – are clearly in evidence on the mizzen mast. Shroud cleats can also be added to these pins, according to Cleveley. He also shows the forecastle rail carrying other belaying pins. This demonstrates that belaying pins were used extensively on *Royal Caroline*, perhaps earlier than their official recognition, and we feel fully justified in placing a half dozen on a crosspiece between the main topsail sheet bitts and a few more between the fore topsail bitts.

The plans in the National Maritime Museum show two large cleats on either side of the ship and there is the usual series of timberheads found on all English ships of this period. This is just about the total number of belaying points available for the ship's rigging. *Royal Caroline* was at a great disadvantage in this respect compared to other ships of her class because a good part of her main deck was taken up by the main cabin and completely bereft of belaying points. Even without the rigging to studding sails, which were belayed wherever possible (on top of the other ropes in the absence of free points), it was difficult to find a convenient point for each rope.

The arrangement of the ropes obviously varied according to the type of ship and with the passage of time and, very considerably, with the evolution of masting and rigging. However, it was said that a seaman finding himself at night on the deck of an unknown ship could find the correct rope to carry out an order by feeling his way. This is certainly an exaggeration but it expresses the theory of the arrangement, which can be summarised as follows: the ropes which were usually employed together had to be arranged so that the seamen did not get in each other's way, and, compatibly with this, an arrangement was favoured which helped the crew to memorise their positions; for example, the lower, topsail and topgallant bowlines were arranged in a certain sequence on a pin rack. Ropes subject to great strain needed stout anchorage points, while simple fixing points were sufficient for the others. Belaying points had to be arranged in such a way as to avoid complicated leads and make the ropes run smartly without crossing others: in a nutshell, 'shipshape', *ie* orderly, logical and aesthetically pleasing.

Naturally there is no written evidence to indicate where individual ropes were belayed at the time of *Royal Caroline* and it would be difficult to find such a source for the whole age of sail, unless perhaps for the latter period. Lees has given some examples of belaying plans from his examination of models. On the basis of this, and taking into account the yacht's special features, we have prepared a belaying plan. The ropes are identified by a three-figure code where each number and position have a meaning. This system, as opposed to a progressive numeration, means that a rope can be identified without the need to refer to an explanatory list. This has been done to help those who may build a model of *Royal Caroline* and find themselves faced with the classic problem of arranging the ropes on deck.

The first number in the three-figure code indicates the mast to which the rope belongs:

1 – bowsprit
2 – foremast
3 – mainmast
4 – mizzen mast

The second number describes the kind of sail to which the rope belongs (lower, top- or topgallant); the first three refer to square sails, and the others to fore and aft sails:

1 – course
2 – topsail
3 – topgallant sail
4 – lower staysail
5 – topmast staysail
6 – jib or middle staysail
7 – flying jib or topgallant staysail
8 – mizzen sail

In our reconstruction, *Royal Caroline* carries only a lower staysail on the mizzen; she does not have a middle staysail or a flying jib. The code could easily be used to identify the ropes on ships with a more complicated rigging.

The third number indicates the specific rope according to the following scheme:

a) square sails (second figure from 1 to 3)

1 – tie and halyard, or jeers
2 – lift
3 – parrel or truss
4 – brace
5 – sheet
6 – clueline
7 – buntline
8 – leechline
9 – bowline
0 – tack (to courses; reef tackle to topsails)

b) staysail (second figure from 4 to 7)

1 – halyard

5 – sheet
7 – staysail stay
8 – stay
9 – downhauler
c) mizzen sail (second figure 8)
   1 – halyard
   2 – mizzen lifts
   3 – mizzen parrel
   4 – vang
   5 – sheet
   6 – brails
   9 – bowlines

RIGGING DIMENSIONS

Finally, we should like to give some idea of the thickness of the cordage used to rig ships in the class of *Royal Caroline*. The tables in Steel's *Elements of Rigging* provide all the necessary details, but even for a single type, they are very extensive. We feel it more appropriate to provide a summary here. For example, the thickness of the lanyards, runners or seizings for each separate item of standing or running rigging is not included, as it can be calculated from the thickness of the main cable. In the sailing ship era the thickness was given according to circumference and Steel naturally gives it in inches. Rope sizes progressed in a half-inch steps from the half-inch marline to the 19-inch stay – the largest size for three-deckers. One can understand the preference for circumference instead of diameter. All that was needed to measure it was a piece of twine with knots at ½-inch intervals, which the rigger could carry in his pocket, while a bulkier tool, no matter how simple, would have been needed to measure the diameter. Nowadays it is easier for us to speak of diameter, so we have converted Steel's measurements to diameters and expressed them in centimetres to one decimal point. So in examining the thickness of the standing rigging, we begin, like the riggers, from the bowsprit:

Gammoning	2.0
Bowsprit shrouds	4.0
Bobstays	4.8
Shrouds of jibboom	2.4
Lanyard of bowsprit shrouds	2.0

The thickness of the standing rigging of the other masts is shown in Table 2.

The lanyards of the shrouds were half the diameter of the shroud while lanyards of stays were a little finer, since the heart used to set up the stays allowed more turns than could be given by a three-hole deadeye, the traditional means for setting up shrouds.

The bights of the shrouds around the deadeyes were seized with a 0.8cm marlin on the main and foremast shrouds and a proportionally finer one for the others. Steel tells us that the first two seizings were done with this diameter of rope while the third was one-quarter thinner. The seizings of the stays were proportionately thicker. A rule of thumb is that the rope used for seizing measured one-eighth of the cable to be seized.

One rigging item which was not in proportion to the size of the ship was the ratlines because they were always related to a man's weight. The rope used for this was, according to Steel, 1.2cm for the lower masts and 0.8cm for the topmasts. The topgallant shrouds did not have ratlines. Ratlines at the mizzen mast were the same thickness as those for the main topmast.

The tie blocks of lower yards were lashed to the mast by several turns of

TABLE 2: DIAMETERS OF STANDING RIGGING

	Fore (cm)	Main (cm)	Mizzen (cm)
Lower masts			
Shrouds	6.0	6.0	3.6
Stays	8.9	9.3	4.4
Stay collar	4.4	4.8	–
Catharpin	3.2	3.2	–
Topmasts			
Shrouds			
Backstays	3.6	3.6	2.4
Stays	4.0	4.4	2.8
Collar (of block on lower mast)	3.6	3.6	2.0
Staysail stay	2.4	3.0	–
Collar (of block on lower mast)	1.6	2.0	–
Topgallant masts			
Shrouds	2.0	2.0	1.2
Backstays	2.0	2.0	1.2
Stays	2.4	2.4	1.6

TABLE 3: DIAMETERS OF RUNNING RIGGING TO LOWER YARDS

	Fore and main (cm)	Mizzen (cm)
Tie	6.0	slings 2.8
Runner of halyard	2.4	–
Lift	2.4	1.6
Parrel	4.0	2.4
Pendant of braces	3.2	1.6
Runner of braces	2.4	1.2
Sheet	3.6	–
Clueline	2.0	–
Buntline	1.6	–
Leechline	2.0	–
Bowline	2.4	–
Tack	4.4	–

TABLE 4: DIAMETERS OF RUNNING RIGGING TO TOPMAST YARDS

	Fore and main (cm)	Mizzen (cm)
Tie	3.6	1.4
Runner of halyard	2.0	1.6
Lift	2.0	1.2
Parrel	2.0	1.2
Pendant of braces	2.8	1.6
Sheet	3.6	2.4
Clueline	2.0	1.2
Buntline	1.6	1.2
Leechline	1.6	1.2
Bowline	2.0	1.2
Reef tackle	2.0	1.2

2.4cm rope which ran through the eye of the long strops which carried the blocks and through a stop cleat nailed to the masthead. The strop of the large single block in the centre of the yard was double, made of 4cm cable served all over while the strops of the two blocks lashed to the mast head were 3.6cm. The yard arm tackle pendants were 4cm and carried a long-tackle coaked block paired with a single block which was also coaked. The runner was 2.4cm in diameter.

TABLE 5: **DIAMETERS OF RUNNING RIGGING TO TOPGALLANT YARDS**

	Fore and main (cm)	Mizzen (cm)
Tie	2.0	1.6
Runner of halyards	1.2	–
Lifts	2.0	1.2
Parrel	1.2	0.8
Pendant of braces	2.0	–
Runner	1.2	0.8
Sheet (see topmast lifts)	–	–
Cluelines	1.2	0.8
Bowlines	1.2	0.8

TABLE 6: **RUNNING RIGGING TO HEADSAILS AND MIZZEN**

	Spritsail (cm)		Mizzen yard (cm)
Slings	3.6	Jeers (double strop)	2.8
Standing lifts	2.4	Runner of jeers	2.8
Lifts	2.0	Parrel	2.4
Pendants of braces	2.4	Sheet	2.4
Runner	1.6	Vang pendant	2.4
Sheets	2.8	Runner of vangs	1.6
Cluelines	1.6	Bowlines	2.0
Buntlines	1.6	Brails	1.6
		Tack	1.2

The tie of the topsail yards was fitted with two single blocks and one double one of 37 cm (the double block on the yard as in drawing H11). The strop of these blocks measured 3.2cm. The halyards were formed of flat thin blocks hooked onto eyebolts on the chainwales on either side of the ship. The mizzen topsail tie was single.

The standing lifts of the spritsail yard were fitted with a pair of 25cm diameter deadeyes set up by a 1.2cm lanyard. They served to block the spritsail yard in a certain position to withstand buffeting by the sea. The standing lift cable was knotted like bowsprit horses to make it easier to grip but we have no idea in which situations this might have been useful.

Running rigging to the staysails consisted of fairly light ropes. The greatest strain, when these sails were in the wind, was transferred by the hanks to the stay or staysail stay that it was attached to. The sheets and the halyard were the strongest ropes. They ranged from 2.4cm for the sheet of the mizzen staysail (which was small in area but could be used as a storm sail in bad weather) to 1.2cm for topgallant staysails.

The halyards were from 2.0 to 1.2cm (the latter for the mizzen topmast staysail). The downhauler measured 1.2cm on bigger staysails and 0.8 on the smaller ones. The tack was the same thickness as the halyard if it did not consist of a simple marlin passed several times between the tack of the sail and the belaying point.

Blocks. We have seen that the thickness of ropes in English cordage went in half-inch circumference steps. This corresponds roughly to 4mm in diameter. Block sizes, according to Steel, were at intervals of 1 inch in length, *ie* there were blocks of 6, 7 and 8 inches in length. The size of the block was in proportion to the diameter of the runner (the rope which ran through the sheave of the block). These proportions are given in drawing H21 and can be

RIGGING KEY

Course	Spritsail	Fore	Main	Mizzen
Jeers (or tie/halyard)	111	211	311	–
Lift	112	212	312	412
Parrel (or slings to spritsail)	113	213	313	413
Brace	114	214	314	414
Sheet	115	215	315	–
Clueline	116	216	316	–
Buntline	117	217	317	–
Leechline	–	218	318	–
Bowline	–	219	319	–
Tack	–	210	310	–
Topsails		**Fore**	**Main**	**Mizzen**
Tie/halyard		221	321	421
Lift		222	322	422
Parrel		223	323	423
Brace		224	324	424
Sheet		225	325	425
Clueline		226	326	426
Buntline		227	327	427
Leechline		228	328	428
Bowline		229	329	429
Reef tackle		220	320	420
Topgallant sails		**Fore**	**Main**	**Mizzen**
Tie/halyard		231	331	431
Lift		232	332	432
Parrel		233	333	433
Brace		234	334	434
Sheet*		–	–	–
Clueline		236	336	436
Bowline		239	339	439
* see topsail lift				
Staysails		**Fore**	**Main**	**Mizzen**
Lower staysail				
Halyard		–	–	441
Sheet		–	–	445
Tack		–	–	440
Downhauler		–	–	449
Stay		248	348	448
Topsail staysail				
Halyard		251	351	451
Sheet		255	355	455
Tack		250	350	450
Downhauler		259	359	459
Staysail stay		257	357	–
Stay		258	358	458
Jib				
Halyard		261		
Sheet		265		
Tack		260		
Downhauler		269		
Inhauler		269a		
Outhauler		269b		
Staysail stay		267		
Mizzen sail				**Mizzen**
Halyard				481
Mizzen lift				482
Mizzen parrel				483
Vang				484
Sheet				485
Brails				486
Bowline				489

This key applies to all the rigging drawings in section H. In the belaying plan (H25), where the rope was belayed symmetrically on both sides of the ship, the code number is underlined and, as a rule, the corresponding belaying point on the other side is free. Some belaying pins and eyebolts are left free for studding sail rigging and for the hundreds of jobs needed to control a sailing ship, of which we have given only a few examples.

summarised as follows: the diameter of the pulley in normal blocks was from 4.5 to 5 times the diameter of the runner. This proportion had proved to limit wear on the rope. So the total block length is nine to ten times the diameter of the runner. The other block dimensions can be easily derived from this figure.

One can reach a good approximation of both the thickness of the runner and the length of the block from the size of the pendant. It must be remembered that in rigging there is no sense in exaggerating the thickness of one of the component ropes. The most economical arrangement is when both of them are of roughly the same strength. The resistance of a rope varies in proportion to the square of its diameter, but, in the case of tackles, the strain was divided up between the various turns of the runner, while the pendant took it all. To take into account the friction which reduced the mechanical performance of the tackle system made of blocks, the riggers made tackles with runners whose diameters were from half to two-thirds that of the pendant. Blocks were selected according to the diameter of the runner. We are concerned here with tackles and not just simple lead blocks. The difference is considerable because when a block is used simply to lead the rope, the strain is not divided between the turns of the runner but is borne directly by it. In this case, the diameter of the runner tended to equal that of the pendant but, in general, it was slightly less, for the purposes of flexibility.

As for the deadeyes, they were five times the diameter of the shroud or stay to which they belonged, while the stay hearts were four to four-and-a-half times the diameter of their respective cables. These are approximate measurements but they are a useful guide for anyone who wishes to reconstruct the ship's rigging in detail.

Sources

AUBIN, NICOLAS *Dictionnaire de Marine*, Amsterdam 1702.

DE BONNEFOUX PMJ *Le Manoeuvrier Complet*, Paris 1852.

BROOKE, JOHN *King George III*, London 1972.

CANO, THOME *Arte de fabricar y aparejar Navios*, Seville 1611.

CHAPMAN, FREDERICK AF *Architectura Navalis Mercatoria*, Stockholm 1768

CHARNOCK, JOHN *Biographia Navalis*, 5 vols, London 1937.

COSTA, GIANCARLO *Angeli di legno*, Milan 1978.

D'ARCY LEVER *The Young Sea Officer's Sheet Anchor*, London 1819; reprinted 1963.

DUDLEY, ROBERT *L'Arcano del Mare*, Florence 1676.

DUHAMEL DE MONCEAU *Traité de la Fabrique des Manoeuvres pour le Vaisseau, ou, l'Art de la Corderie*, Paris 1747.

FALCONER, WILLIAM *A Universal Dictionary of the Marine*, London 1780; reprinted 1970.

GAVIN, CM *Royal Yachts*, London 1932.

GARDINER, ROBERT 'The First English Frigates', *The Mariner's Mirror* 61 (1975), 2.

– 'The Frigate Design of 1755–57', *The Mariner's Mirror* 63 (1977), 1.

– 'Les fregates françaises et la Royal Navy', *Petit Perroquet* 21 (1977) 24 (1978).

DE GROOT – VORSTMANN *Sailing Ships – Prints by the Dutch Masters*, Maarsen (1980).

HAGEDORN, BERNHARD *Die Entwicklung der wichtigsten Schiffstypen*, Berlin 1914.

HANSEN, HJ *Galionsfiguren*, Oldenburg 1979.

HARLAND, JOHN & MYERS, MARK *Seamanship in the Age of Sail*, London 1984.

HAYWARD, EDWARD *The Sizes and Lengths of Rigging*, London 1956; reprinted 1967.

HUSSEY, FRANK *The Royal Harwich*, Ipswich 1972.

HUTCHINSON, WILLIAM *A treatise on Practical Seamanship*, London 1777; reprinted 1979.

IMPERATO, FEDERICO *Arte Navale*, vol I, *Attrezzatura e manovra*, Milan 1929.

KOESTER, AUGUST *Modelle alter Segelschiffe*, Berlin 1926.

LAIRD CLOWES, GS *Sailing Ships: Their History and Development*, 2 vols, London 1931.

LAVERY, BRIAN, *The Ship of the Line*, 2 vols, London 1983, 1984.

– *The 74-gun ship Bellona*, London 1985.

LEES, JAMES *The Masting and Rigging of English Ships of War 1625–1850*, London 1979.

LESCALLIER, DANIEL *Traité pratique du greément du vaisseau*, Paris 1791.

MANNING, SF *New England Masts and the King's Broad Arrow*, London 1979.

MAY, WE *The Boats of Men of War*, London 1974.

McGOWAN, ALAN *Tiller and Whipstaff*, London 1981.

– 'The Structure of Wooden Hulls', *Five Hundred Years of Nautical Science, 1400–1900*, London 1981.

– *Royal Yachts*, London 1977.

NAISH, GPB *Royal Yachts*, London 1964.

NEDERLANDSCH HISTORISCH SCHEEPSVAART MUSEUM *Beschrijvende Catalogus der Scheepsmodellen 1600–1900*, Amsterdam 1943.

NORTON, PETER *Figureheads*, London 1972.

– *State Barges*, London 1972.

PALACIO, DIEGO GARCIA DE *Instruccion Nautica para Navagar*, Mexico 1587, reprinted 1944.

PLUMB, JH *The First Four Georges*, London 1956.

PURVES, AA *Flags for Ship Modellers and Marine Artists*, London 1950; reprinted 1983.

RITTMEISTER, W & AHRENS, H *Neptuns hoelzerne Engel*, Hamburg 1958.

ROBERTSON, FL *The Evolution of Naval Armament*, London 1921; reprinted 1968.

ROEDING, JH *Allgemeines Woerterbuch der Marine*, Hamburg 1793; reprinted 1969.

RYAN, WR 'Peter the Great's English Yacht', *The Mariner's Mirror*, 69 (1983), 1.

STEEL, DAVID *Elements of Mastmaking, Sailmaking and Rigging*, London 1794; reprinted 1932.

STENGELHOFER, JOHN *Valhalla, The Tresco Ships Figurehead Collection*, London 1984.

STRATICO, SIMONE *Vocabolario di Marina in tre lingue*, Milan 1813.

US NAVAL ACADEMY MUSEUM *HH Rodgers' Collection of Ship Models*, Annapolis 1971.

WAITE, AH *National Maritime Museum Catalogue of Ship Models*, Part 1, London nd.

WILLAUME, BERNARD 'Le yacht hollandais de Charles XI de Suède', *Petit Perroquet* 25 (1979).

WITSEN, NICOLAES *Architectura Navalis et Regimen Nauticum*, Amsterdam 1671; reprinted 1969.

ZIMMERMANN, WERNER 'Farben an Schiffen; Ueberlegungen zur farbigen Ausgestaltung historischer Schiffe', *Das Logbuch* 1986, 1.

The Photographs

All the photographs reproduced in this section were supplied by the author, Sergio Bellabarba, and show his own model of *Royal Caroline*.

2. Broadside view, port side.

3. Starboard bow view from above, showing general arrangement of upper deck.

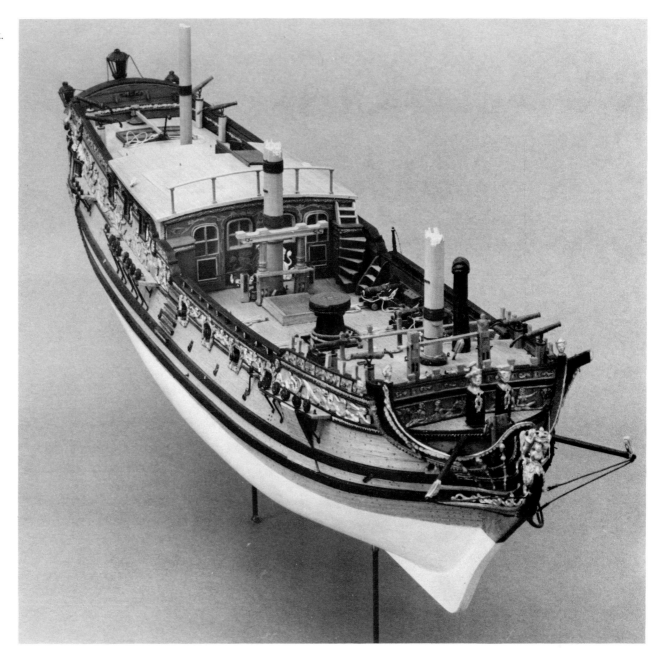

4. Midships view, showing midships bulkhead and boat gallows.

5. View from aft, showing quarter decoration and the poop.

6. Midships view forward, showing capstan, anchor bitt and forecastle.

7. The richly-carved stern.

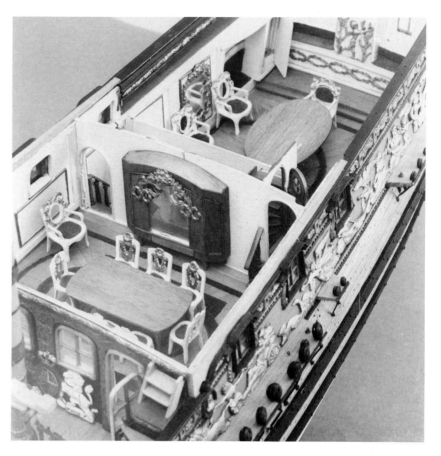

8. Interior view, with the coachroof and decking removed.

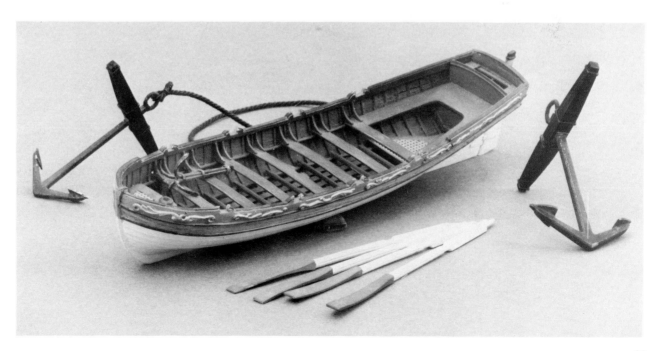

9. The launch, with oars and two anchors.

10. Bow view, showing details of the figurehead group, knightheads and decoration.

11. General view for the port quarter.

The Drawings

All the drawings in this section are by Giorgio Osculati.

A Lines and general arrangement

A1   LINES
A1/1   Sheer elevation (1/96 scale)

A1/2   Body plan aft showing the run of the planking (1/48 scale)

A1/3   Body plan forward

A1/4   Waterlines (1/96 scale)

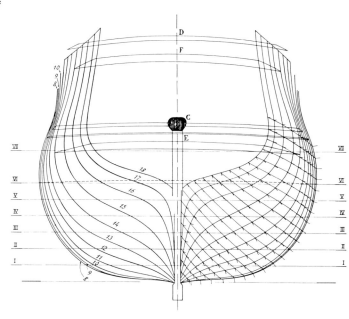

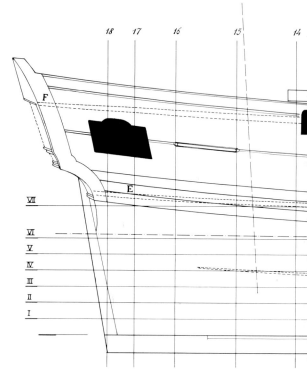

A1/2

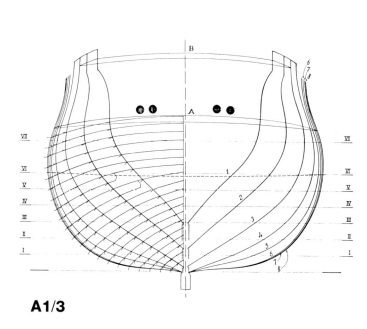

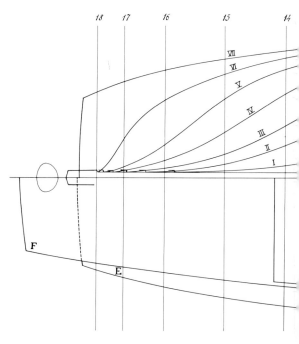

A1/3

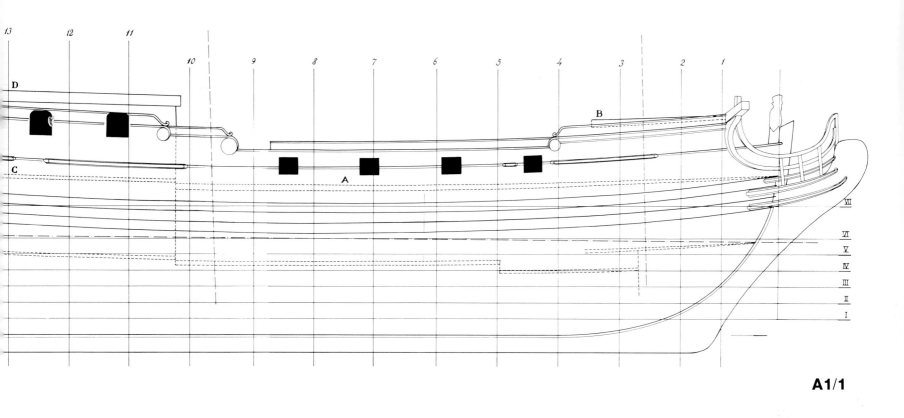

A1/1

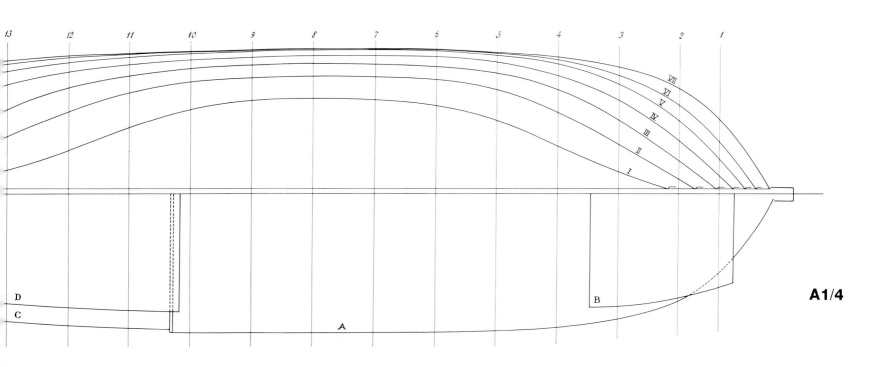

A1/4

A Lines and general arrangement

A2 EXTERNAL ARRANGEMENTS

A2/1 Sheer elevation (1/96 scale)

A2/2 Plan view of weather decks (1/96 scale)

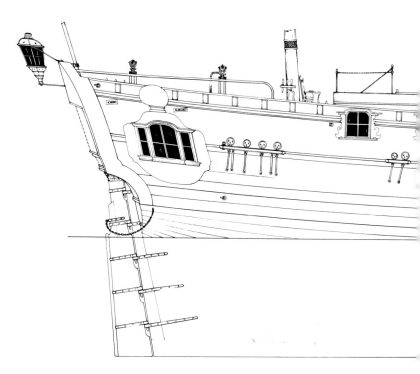

A2/1

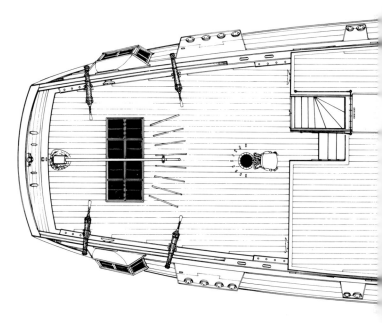

A2/2

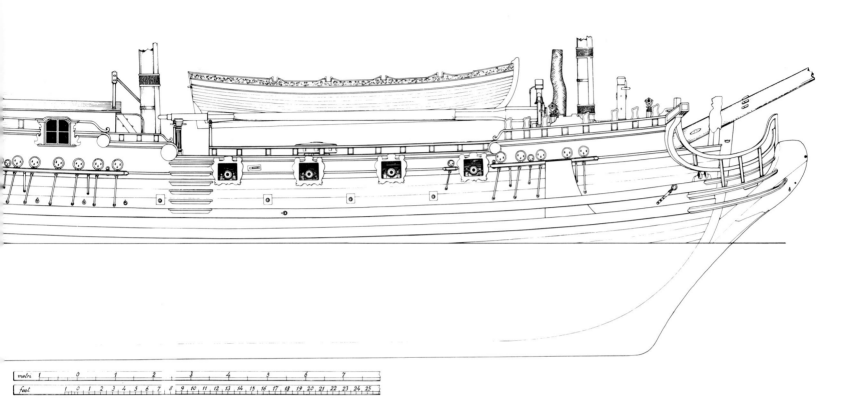

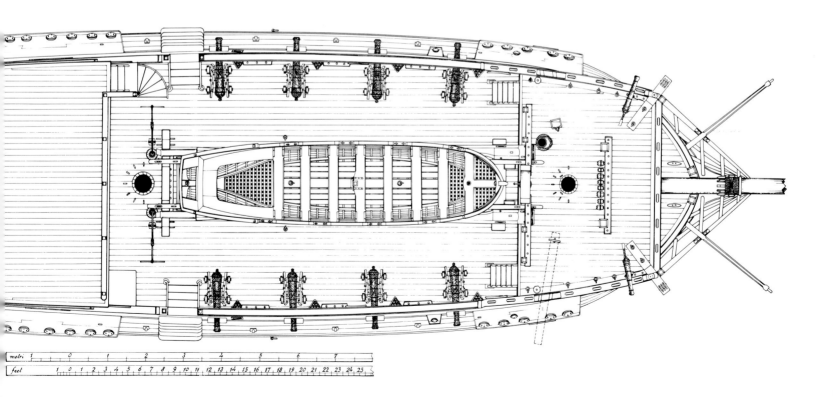

A Lines and general arrangement

A2/3 Aft decorative details (1/48 scale)

A2/4 Forward decorative details (1/48 scale)

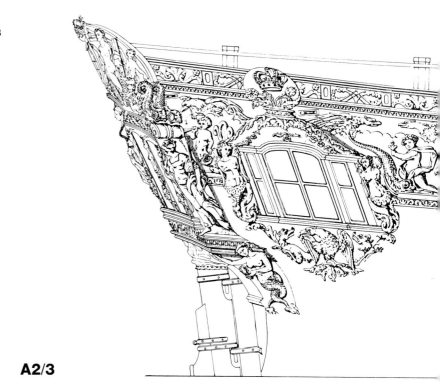

A2/3

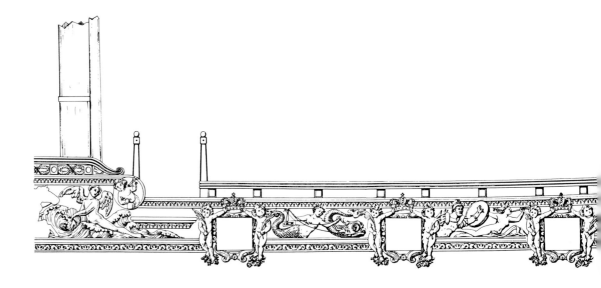

A2/4

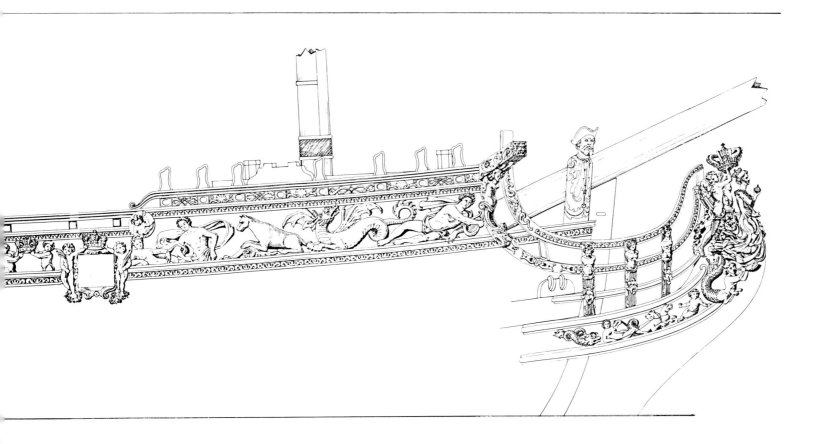

A Lines and general arrangement

A3 INTERNAL ARRANGEMENT
(1/96 scale)

1. Cheese lockers
2. One Captain's servant
3. Two Captain's servants
4. Pease and other stores
5. Scuttle to various store rooms
6. Scuttle to shifting ballast
7. One Captain's servant
8. Two Captain's servants
9. Captain's steward's cabin
10. Three carpenter's mates
11. Captain's storeroom
12. Master's cabin
13. Carpenter's cabin
14. Three seamen
15. Cable tier
16. Three seamen
17. Three seamen
18. Pantry
19. Boatswain's storeroom
20. Carpenter's and gunner's storeroom
21. Two seamen
22. Two seamen
23. One seaman
24. Two seamen
25. Two seamen
26. Boatswain's cabin
27. Gunner's cabin
28. Doctor's cabin
29. Captain's cabin
30. Two midshipmen
31. Master's mates
32. Bread room

A3/1   Plan view of upper deck

A3/2   Plan view of lower deck

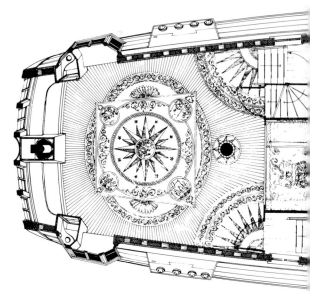

A3/1

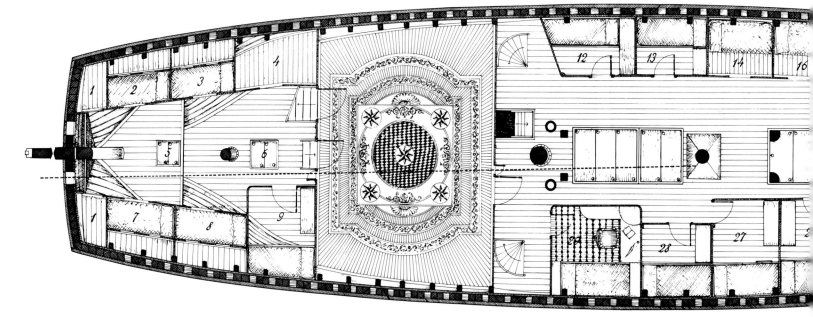

A3/2

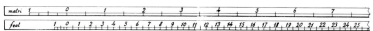

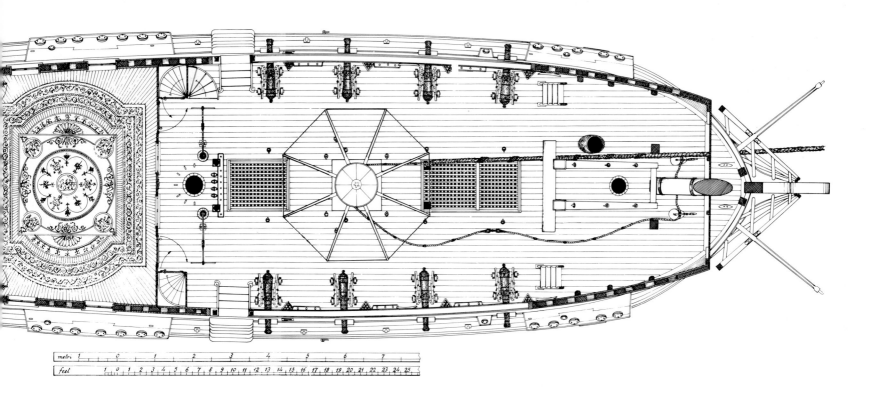

metri 1   0   1   2   3   4   5   6   7
feet   1 0 1 2 3 4 5 6 7 8 9 10 11 12 13 14 15 16 17 18 19 20 21 22 23 24 25

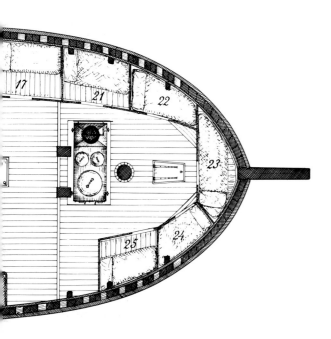

17

21

22

23

25   24

A Lines and general arrangement

A3/3 Longitudinal profile

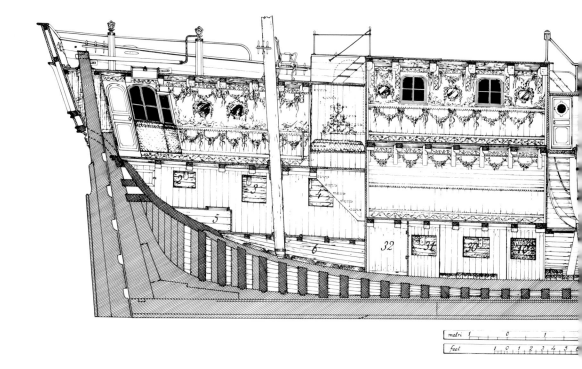

A3/3

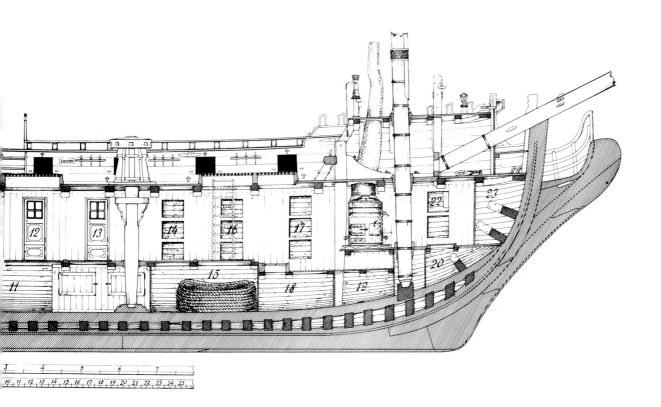

B Construction

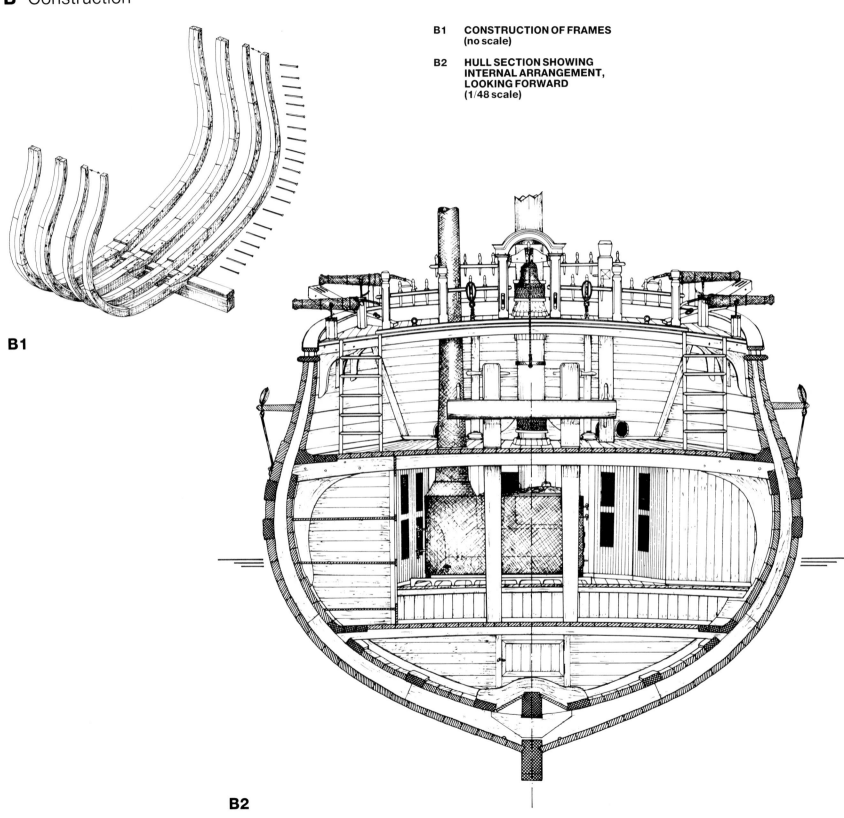

B1 **CONSTRUCTION OF FRAMES**
(no scale)

B2 **HULL SECTION SHOWING
INTERNAL ARRANGEMENT,
LOOKING FORWARD**
(1/48 scale)

B1

B2

B3   HULL SECTION FORWARD OF
THE MAIN MAST, LOOKING AFT
(1/48 scale)

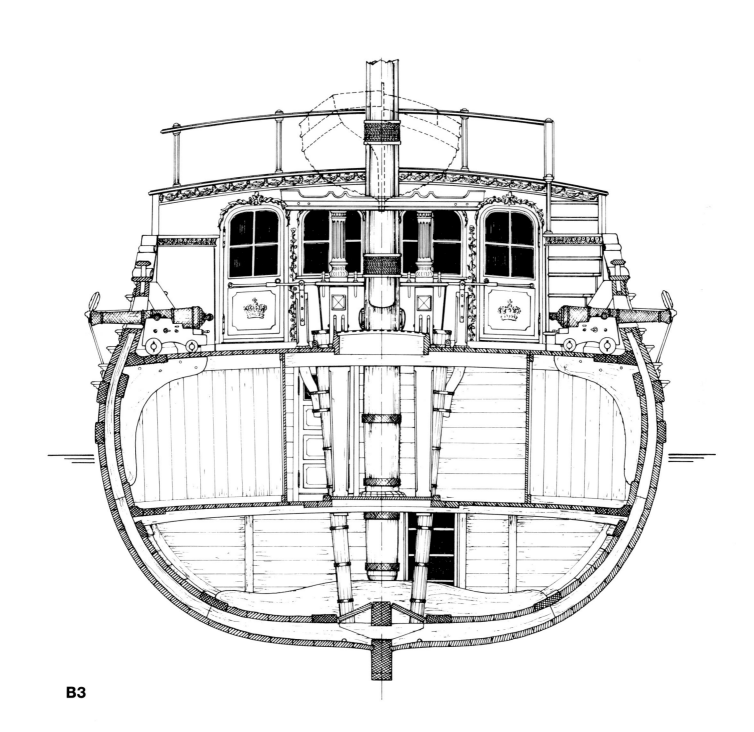

B3

B Construction

**B4 THE STRUCTURE OF THE STERN
(1/48 scale)**
Based on six counter timbers tenoned
into the wind transom; in this case the
wing transom is positioned between
the two lower wales above the stern
ports.

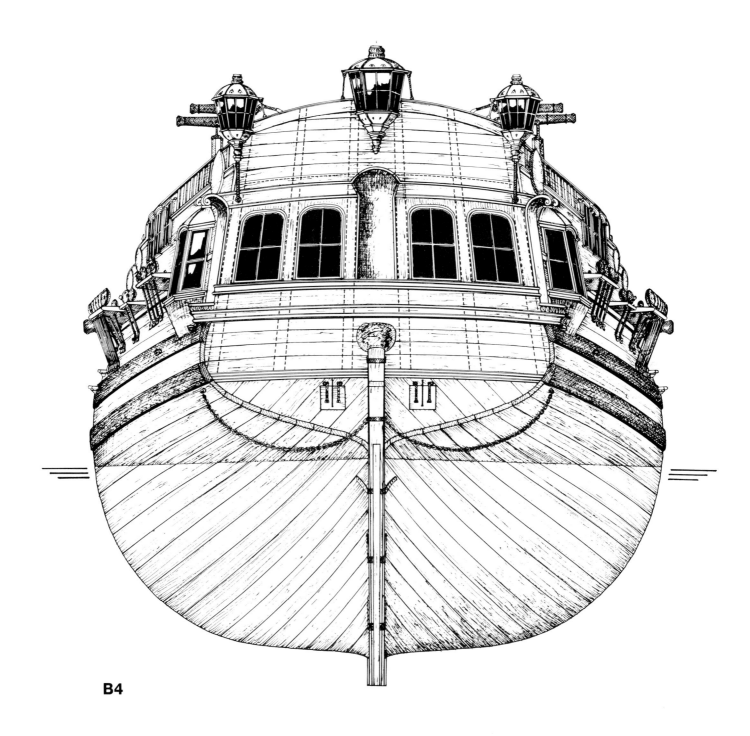

B4

B5 **THE STRUCTURE OF THE BOWS**
(1/48 scale)
The head rails were made of several
pieces of naturally curved wood held
together by mortice and tenons and
dowels.

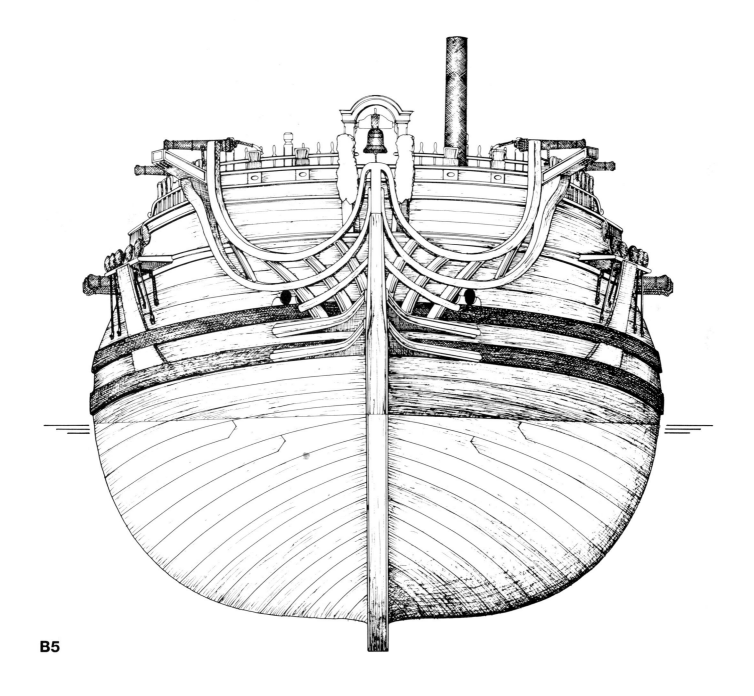

B5

C Fittings

C1/1

C1/2

C1   SCUPPERS

C1/1   One of the four scuppers in the form of a satyr's head for draining the main deck (1/12 scale)
Evidence for the existence of these scuppers is provided only by Cleveley's painting. There must have been another scupper on each side of the mizzen deck, at the foot of the cabin bulkhead.

C1/2   Detail from outboard, showing the satyr's head

C2   THE COMPANION OF THE GREAT CABIN (1/24 scale)
This is another detail furnished by Cleveley, since the plans make no reference to it. Obviously it could be a later addition and the scuppers an oversight.

C2/1   Plan view

C2/2   Athwartship section

C2/3   Fore and aft section

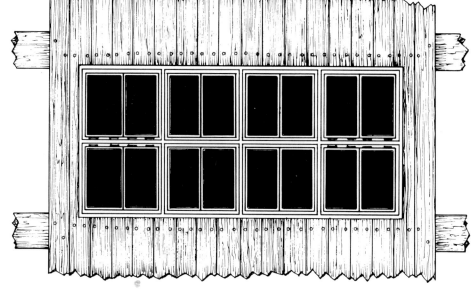

C2/1

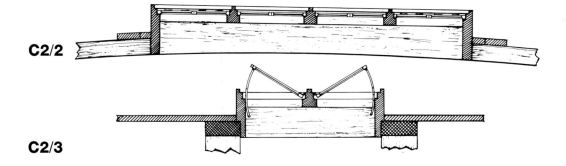

C2/2

C2/3

**C3   THE ANCHOR BITT, WITH THE
      FOREMAST PARTNERS FITTED
      WITH WEDGES (1/24 scale)**

C3/1   Side elevation

C3/2   View from aft

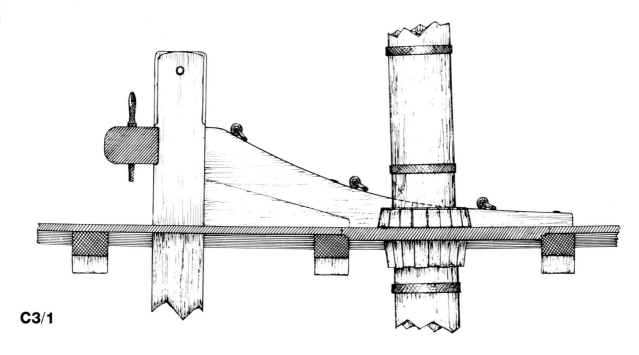

C3/1

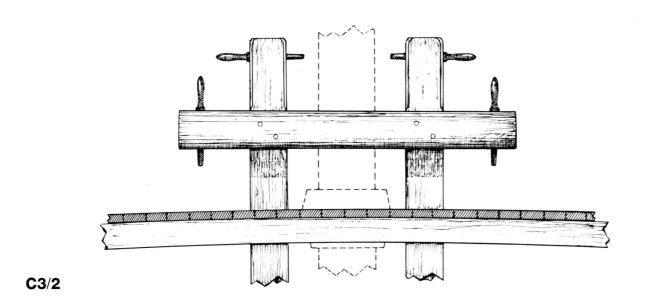

C3/2

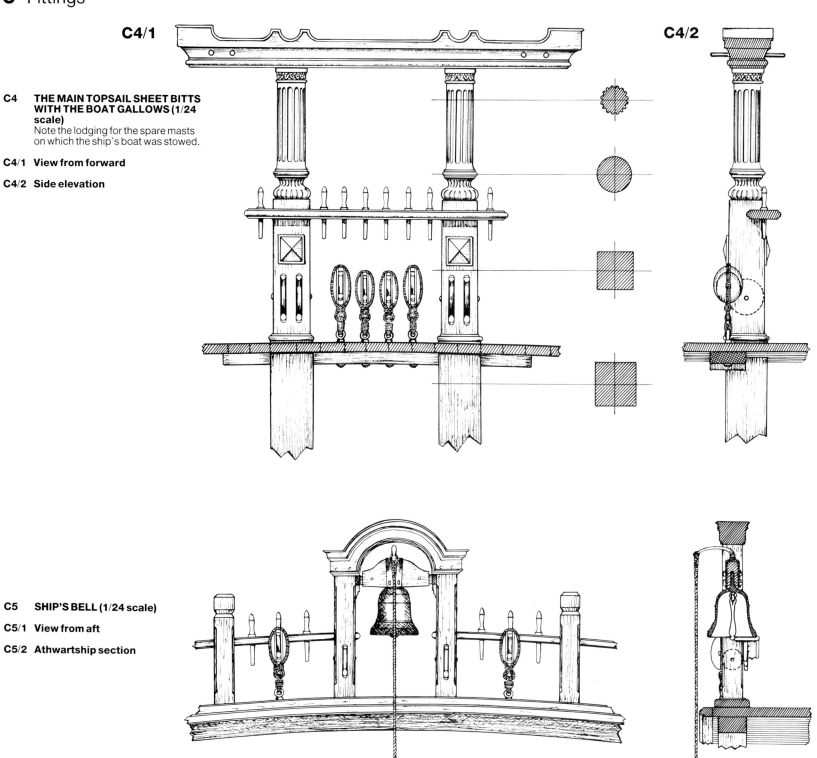

C4/1

C4/2

C4 **THE MAIN TOPSAIL SHEET BITTS WITH THE BOAT GALLOWS (1/24 scale)**
Note the lodging for the spare masts on which the ship's boat was stowed.

C4/1 **View from forward**

C4/2 **Side elevation**

C5 **SHIP'S BELL (1/24 scale)**

C5/1 **View from aft**

C5/2 **Athwartship section**

C5/1

C5/2

C6   FORE SHEET BITTS (1/24 scale)

C6/1   View from forward

C6/2   Plan view

C6/3   Athwartship section

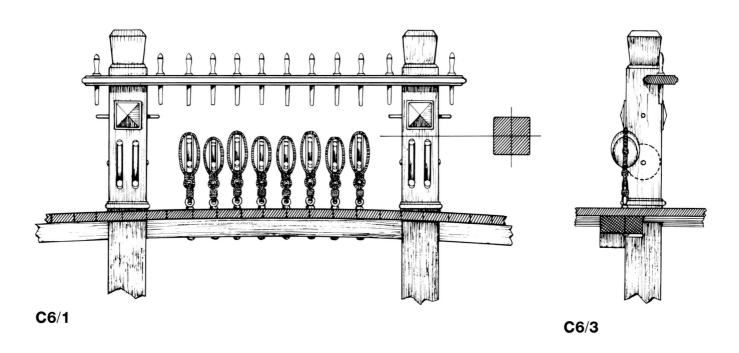

C6/1

C6/3

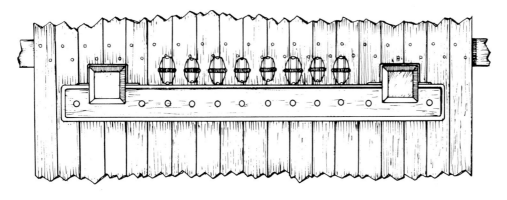

C6/2

C Fittings

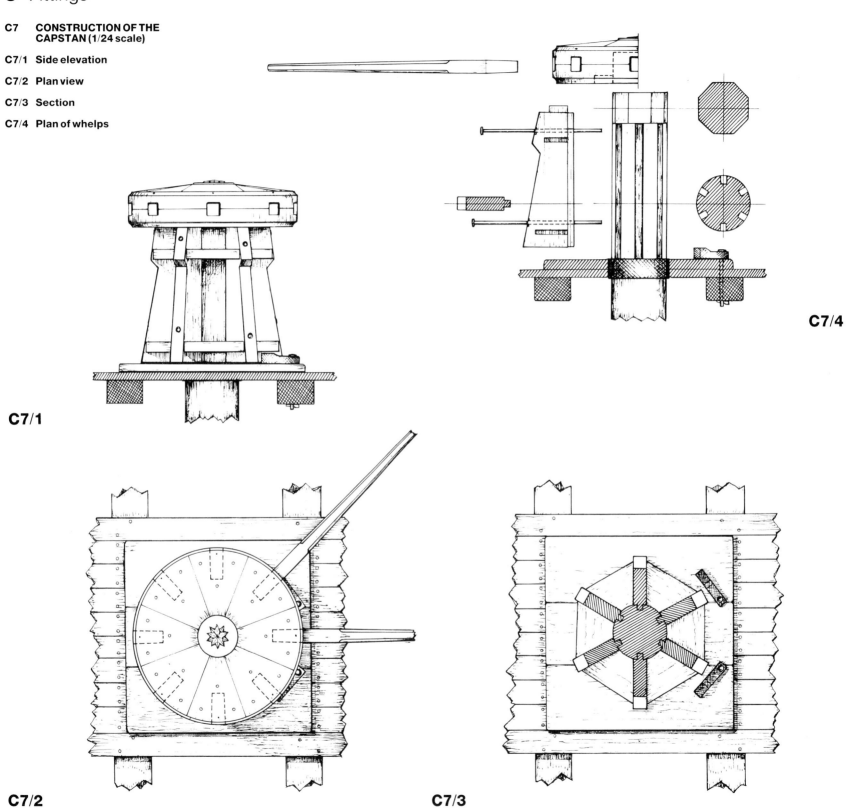

C7/4

C7/1

C7/2

C7/3

64

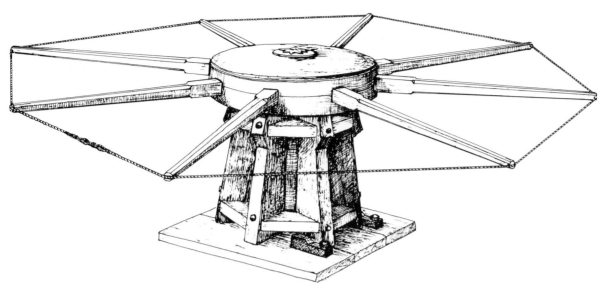

**C7/5 The capstan with the bars in
position (no scale)**
A rope was run round their ends and
pulled taut to keep them in place.

C7/5

C8   ANCHOR TACKLE (1/24 scale)

C8/1 Fish davit, elevation and plan

C8/2 Fish hook and tackle

C8/3 Spanshackle

C8/1

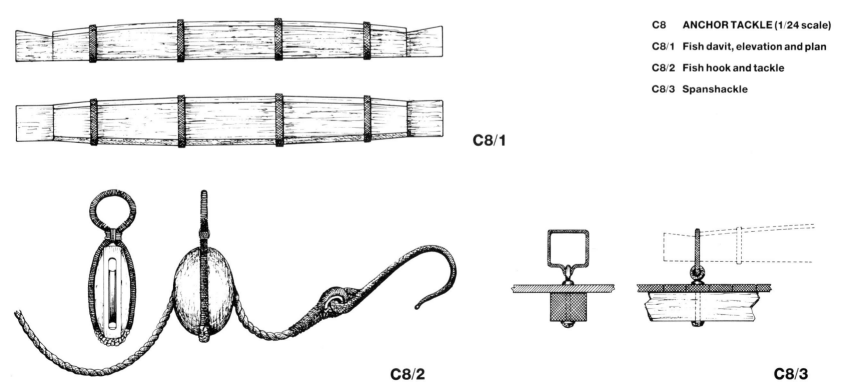

C8/2

C8/3

C Fittings

C8/4 Rigging the fish tackle

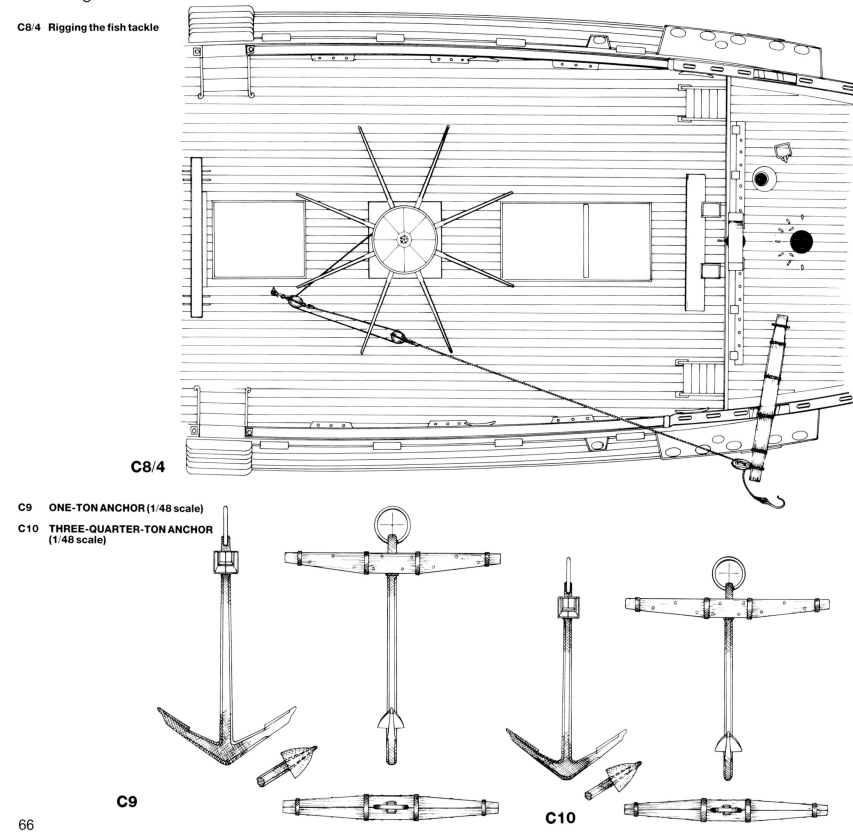

C8/4

C9   ONE-TON ANCHOR (1/48 scale)

C10   THREE-QUARTER-TON ANCHOR
(1/48 scale)

C9

C10

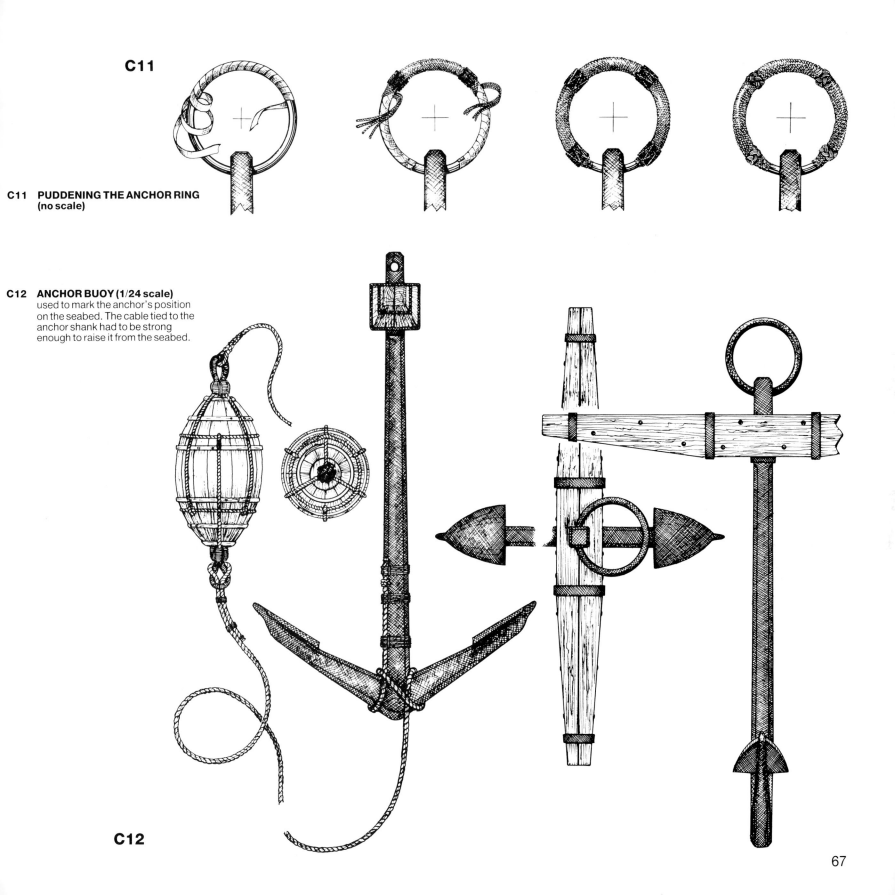

C11

C11 PUDDENING THE ANCHOR RING
(no scale)

C12 ANCHOR BUOY (1/24 scale)
used to mark the anchor's position
on the seabed. The cable tied to the
anchor shank had to be strong
enough to raise it from the seabed.

C12

C Fittings

**C13 METHOD OF ATTACHING THE
ANCHOR CABLE TO THE
ANCHOR** (no scale)

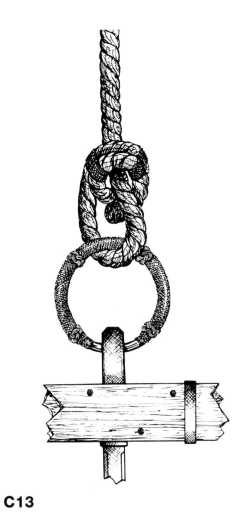

C13

C14 ANCHORS, CABLES AND BUOY
(no scale)

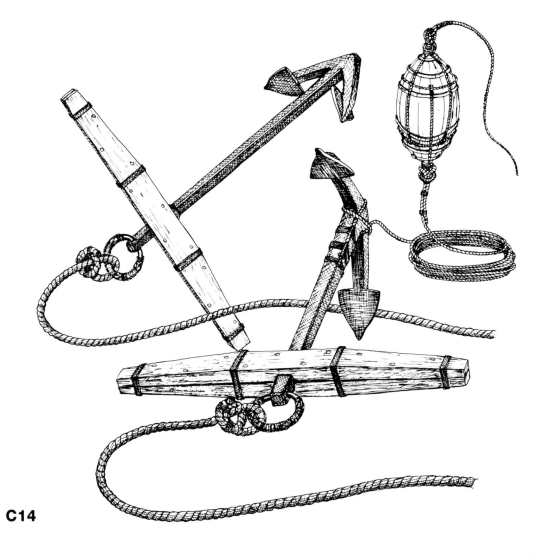

C14

C15

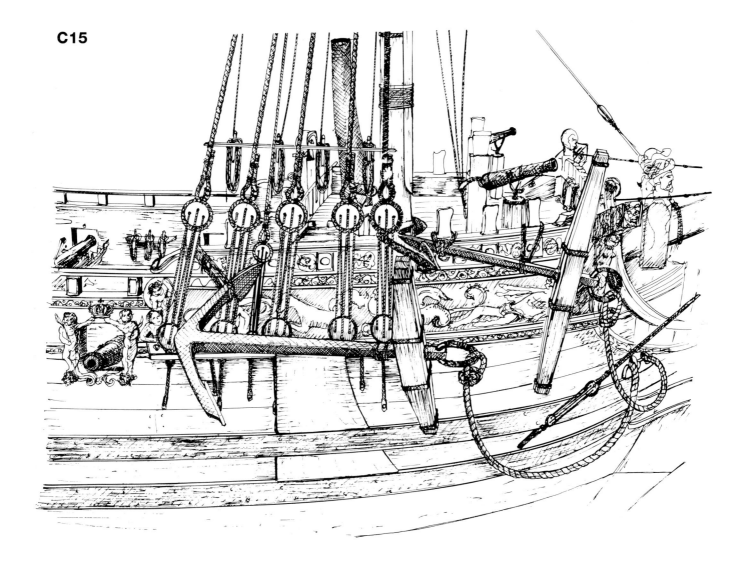

C Fittings

C16 **GRATINGS (1/24 scale)**

C16/1 **Mast hatch**

C16/2 **Fore hatch**

C16/3 **Section of hatchways**

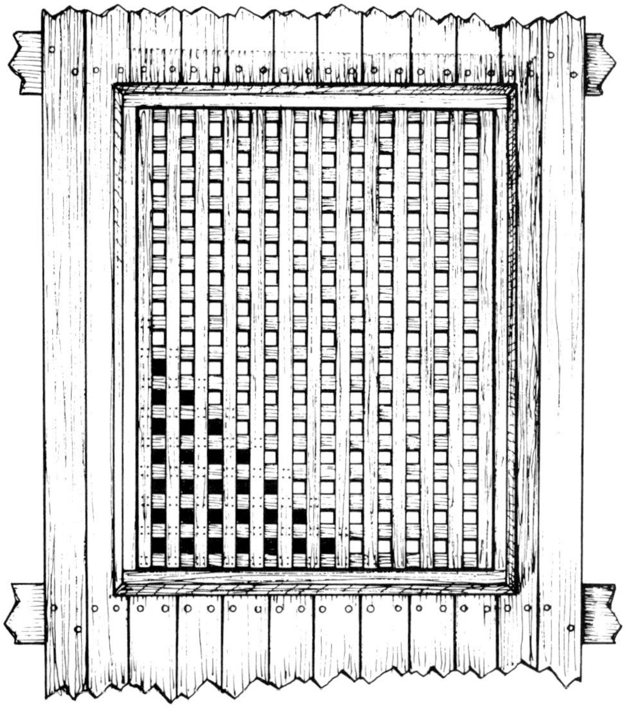

C16/1

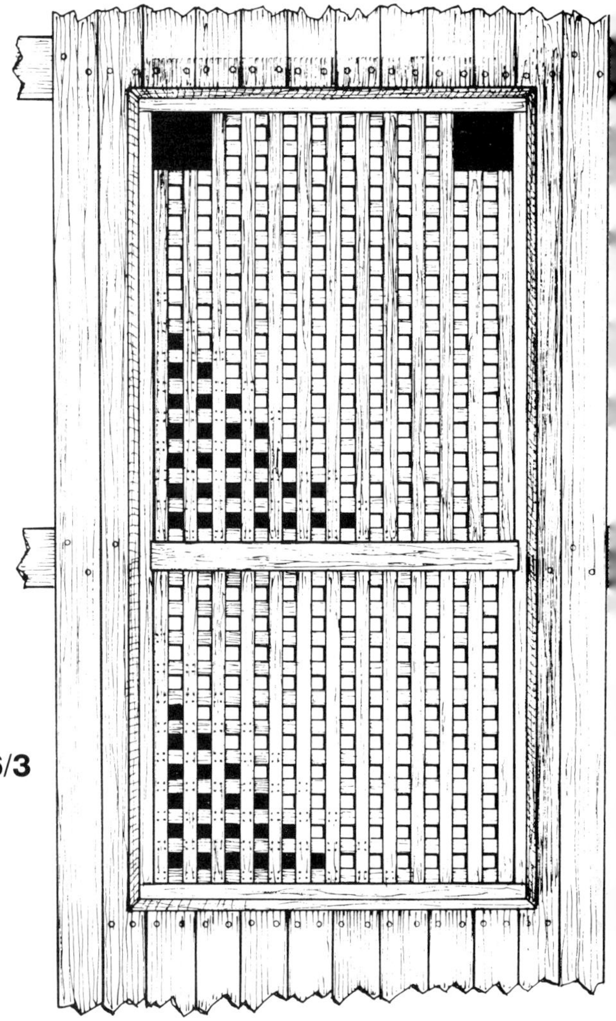

C16/3

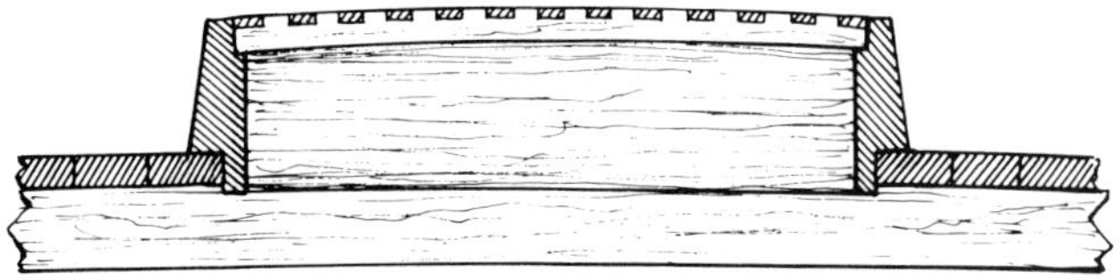

C16/2

C17 **HANDPUMP, CONSISTING OF A SIMPLE LEVER-OPERATED PISTON (1/24 scale)**

C17/1 **Athwartship elevation**

C17/2 **Plan view**

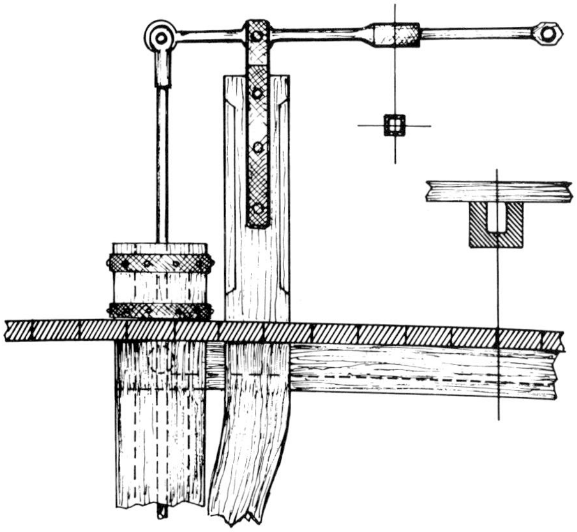

C17/1

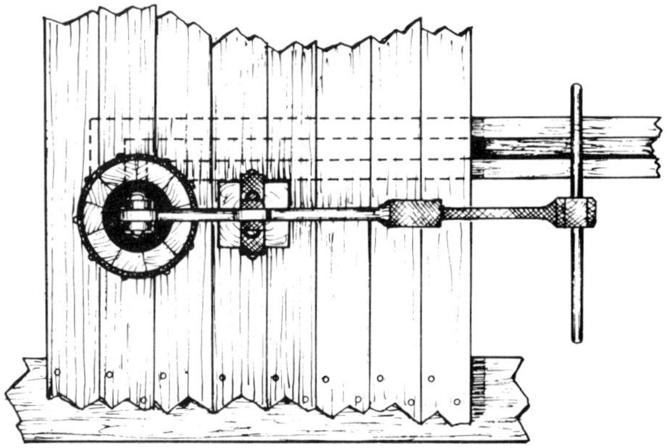

C17/2

C18 **MAIN STERN LANTERN (1/26 scale)**

C18/1 **View from aft**

C18/2 **Side elevation**

C18/3 **Sectional elevation**

C18/4 **Plan view**

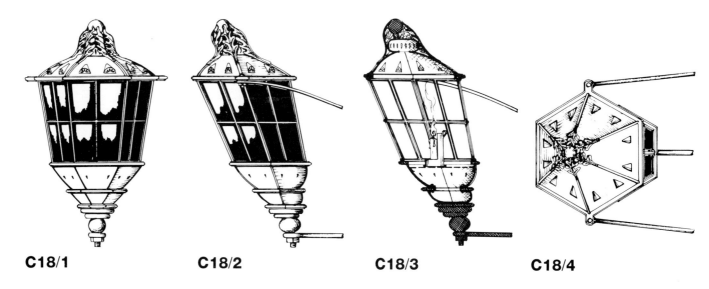

C18/1   **C18/2**   **C18/3**   **C18/4**

C19 **SMALL STERN LANTERNS (1/24 scale)**

C19/1 **View from aft**

C19/2 **Side elevation**

C19/3 **Detail of access hatch (2 x scale)**

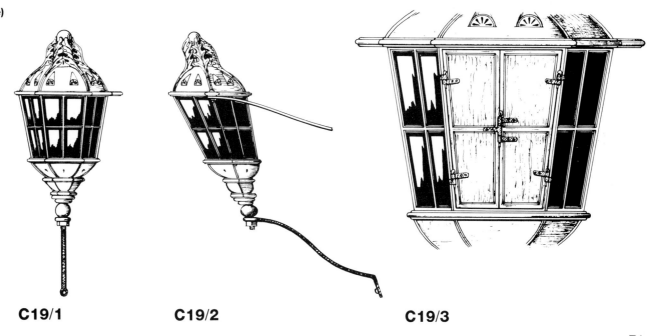

C19/1   **C19/2**   **C19/3**

D Decoration

D1 DECORATION OF THE STERN (1/24 scale)

Neptune and Tethys, the two sea divinities par excellence, are beneath the taffrail. In the central niche, the Queen is represented bearing crown and sceptre. The Neptune and Tethys theme is repeated in the lower frieze, which was probably painted.

D1

**D2 QUARTER GALLERY WITH
VARIOUS CARVINGS (1/24 scale)**

D2

D3/1

D3 BROADSIDE DECORATION (1/24 scale)

D3/1 The first part (aftermost) of the frieze represents Jove grasping his thunderbolts, surrounded by eagles – and Juno on a coach drawn by geese, birds sacred to her.

D3/2 The second part of the frieze, containing an allegory of a cock being crowned is obscure; the cock usually referred to France.

D3/2

D3/3

D3/3 The third section shows Mars's chariot being driven through the waves by a sea nymph.

D3/4

D3/4 A mythological figure sports in the waves; two putti support a crown over the gunport, sirens and marine beasts continue the frieze.

D3/5 The illustration between the two ports seems to refer to the rape of the Sabines.

D3/5

D Decoration

D3/6 This couple could be Venus and Adonis, but if so we cannot explain the presence of the ferocious looking hound which would discourage the slightest approach.

D3/6

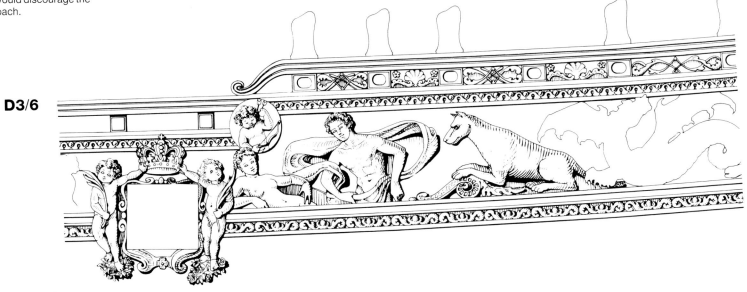

C3/7

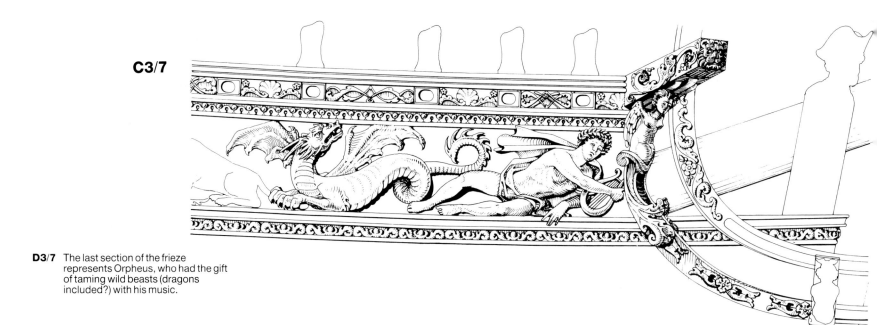

D3/7 The last section of the frieze represents Orpheus, who had the gift of taming wild beasts (dragons included?) with his music.

D4   FIGUREHEAD

D4/1   The figurehead group, in our interpretation of the drawing in *Architectura Navalis Mercatoria* **(1/24 scale)**

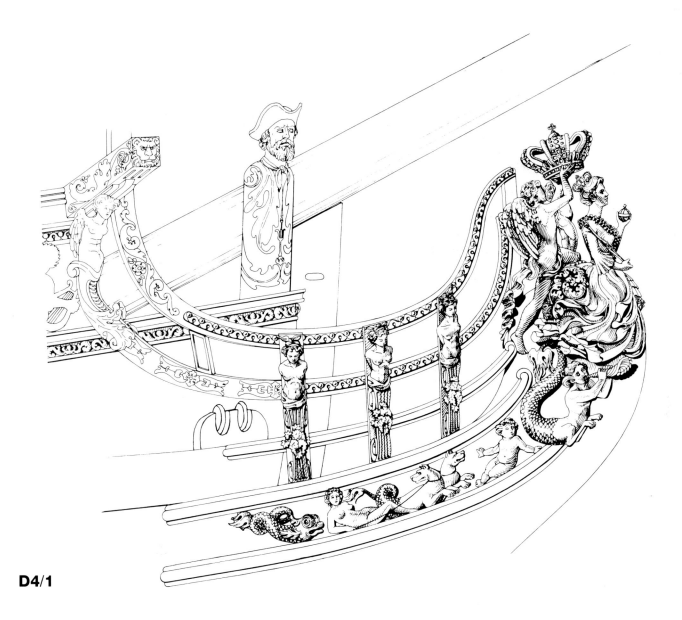

D4/1

D4/2 The figurehead in perspective (no scale)

D4/3 Another perspective view of the figurehead (no scale)

D4/2

D4/3

D4/4 The figurehead illustrated in
Architectura Navalis Mercatoria **(no
scale)**

D5 **DETAIL OF THE MIDSHIPS
BULKHEAD WITH THE ROYAL
COAT OF ARMS (1/24 scale)**

D4/4

D5

E Boats

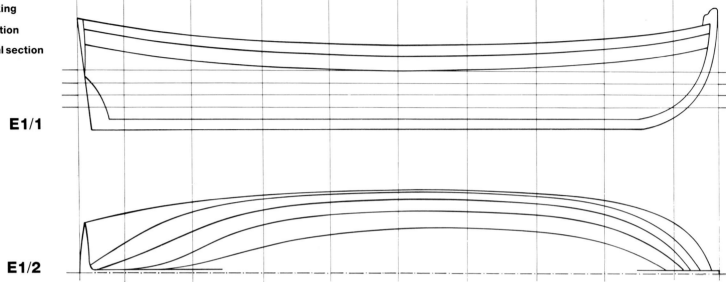

E1/1

E1/2

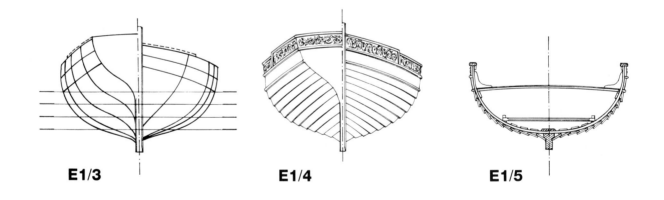

E1/3   **E1/4**   **E1/5**

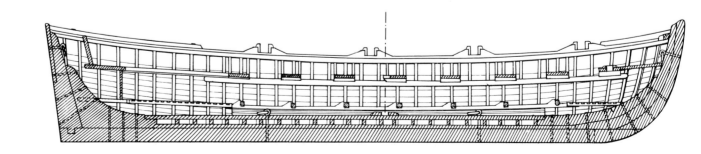

E1/6

E1/8 **Plan view** (in the stern there are six
sockets to take poles for a small
canopy)

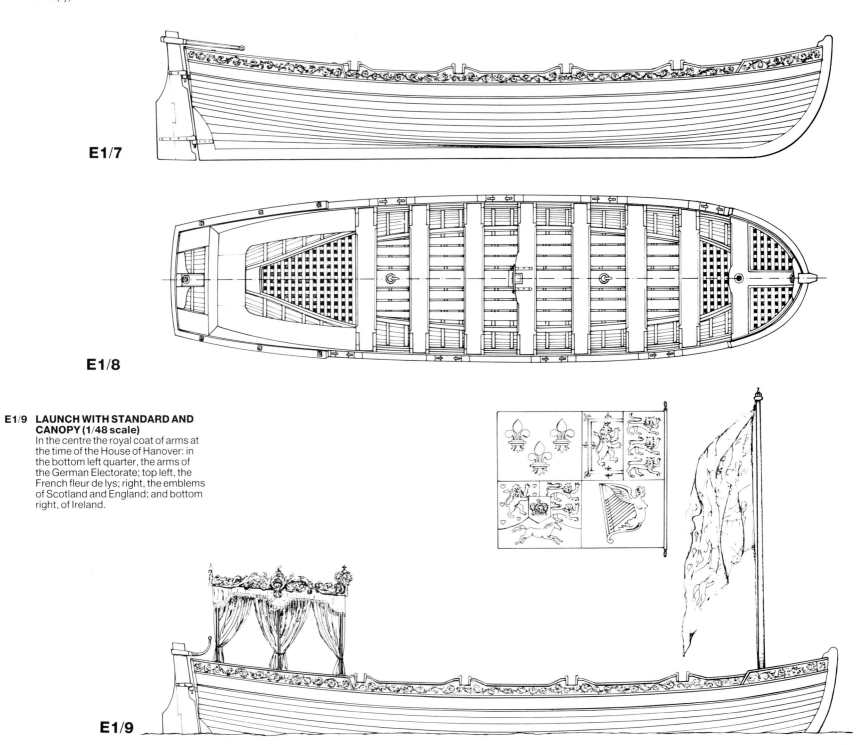

E1/7

E1/8

E1/9 **LAUNCH WITH STANDARD AND
CANOPY (1/48 scale)**
In the centre the royal coat of arms at
the time of the House of Hanover: in
the bottom left quarter, the arms of
the German Electorate; top left, the
French fleur de lys; right, the emblems
of Scotland and England; and bottom
right, of Ireland.

E1/9

E Boats

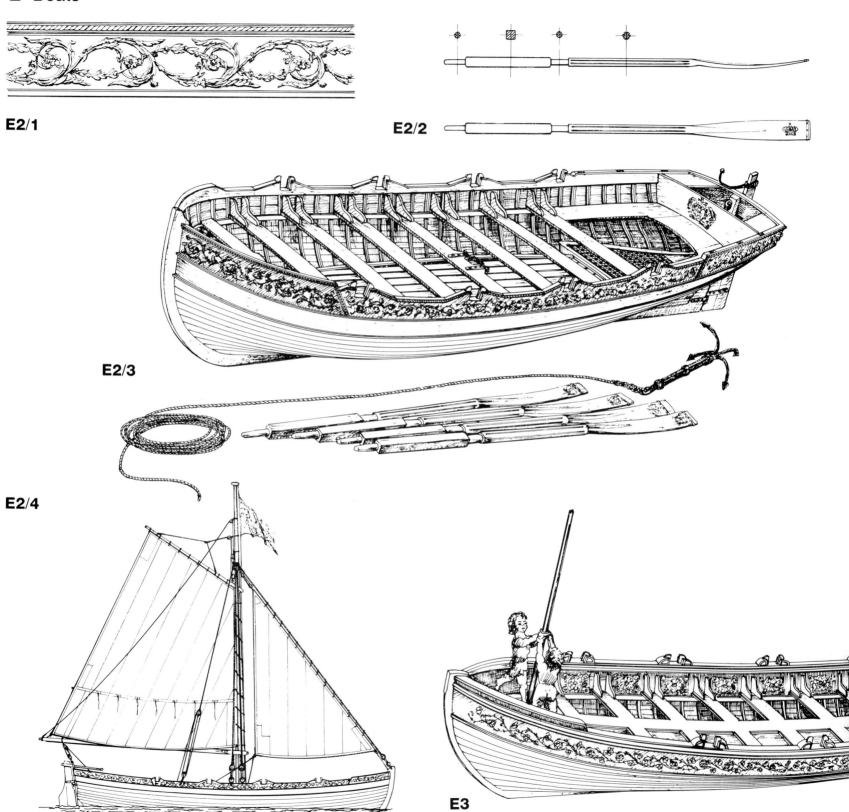

E2/1

E2/2

E2/3

E2/4

E3

E2   DETAILS OF THE LAUNCH

**E2/1   Detail of scrollwork on launch (1/5
scale)**

**E2/2   One of the launch's oars (1/48
scale)**

**E2/3   Perspective view of the launch,
oars and a grapnel (no scale)**

**E2/4   One possible method of rigging
the boat for sail (1/96 scale)**

**E3   PERSPECTIVE VIEW OF BARGE
(no scale)**
A lighter and more decorative craft
than the yawl with which, according to
Cleveley, *Royal Caroline* was
equipped.

**E4   THE WAIST, SEEN FROM AFT,
SHOWING STOWAGE OF THE
BOAT (no scale)**

E4

F Armament

F1 THE 4-POUNDER GUN (1/12 scale)

The maximum range of a 24-pounder gun, with 40-degree elevation, was 3070 metres (Roeding). At a distance of 100 to 200 metres, a 24-pound shot could hole an oak wall one metre thick. The maximum range of these 4-pounders was 1000 metres and their impact was limited. The piece shown here is 20 calibres in length. The weight of the barrel in brass was around 500kg, and around 600kg in iron. The barrel of a 24-pounder weighed 2500 to 3000kg

F1/1 Side elevation

F1/2 Plan view

F1/3 Garland of shot

F1/1

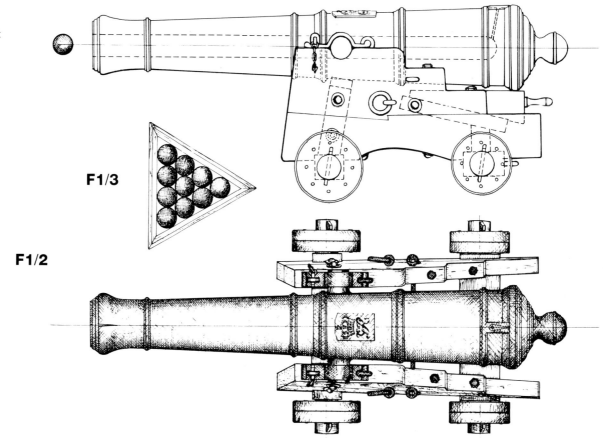

F1/3

F1/2

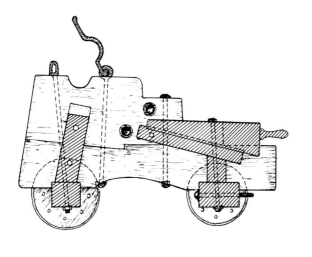

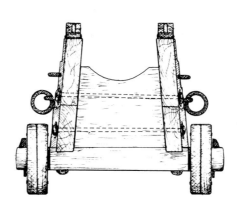

F2/1

F2/2

F2 CARRIAGE FOR 4-POUNDER GUN (1/12 scale)

This type of carraige remained in use for almost three centuries because of its strength and robust simplicity. In spite of all its defects, it could be repaired on board, and it required no great intellect to learn to handle it.

F2/1 Sectional elevation

F2/2 Front view

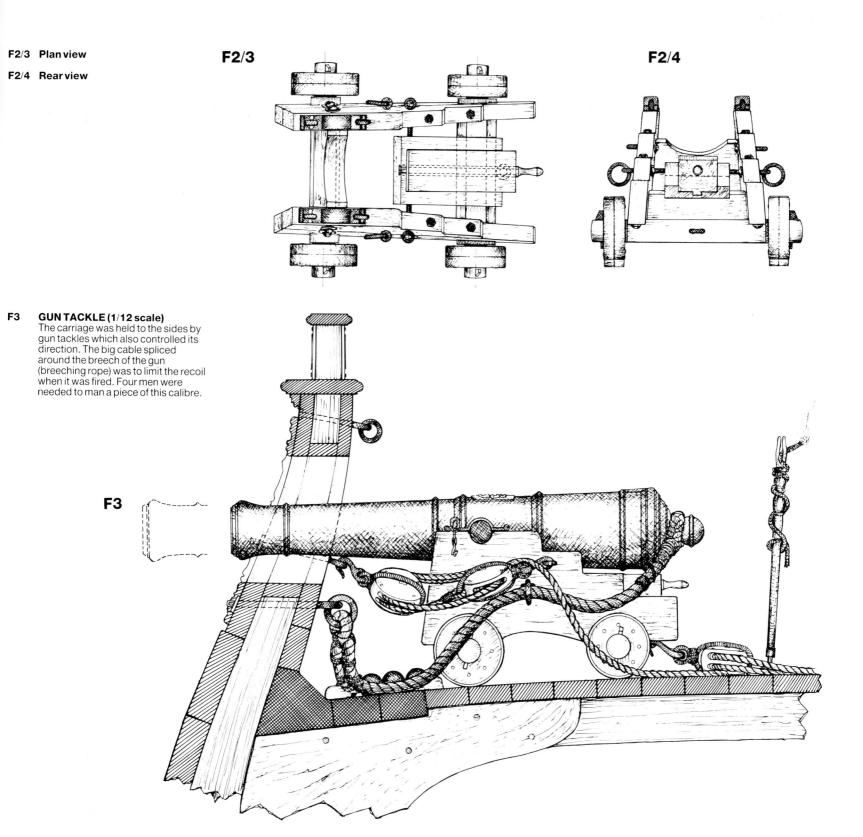

F2/3 Plan view

F2/4 Rear view

F2/3

F2/4

F3   GUN TACKLE (1/12 scale)
The carriage was held to the sides by
gun tackles which also controlled its
direction. The big cable spliced
around the breech of the gun
(breeching rope) was to limit the recoil
when it was fired. Four men were
needed to man a piece of this calibre.

F3

F Armament

F4 **PERSPECTIVE VIEW OF 4-POUNDER (no scale)**

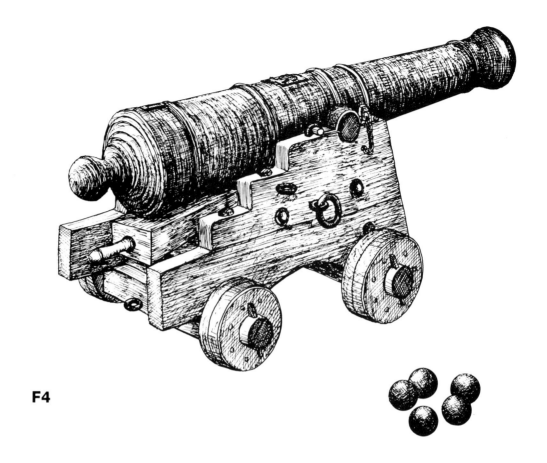

F4

F5 **HALF-POUNDER SWIVEL GUN (1/12 scale)**

F5/1 Side elevation

F5/2 Plan view

F5/3 Front view

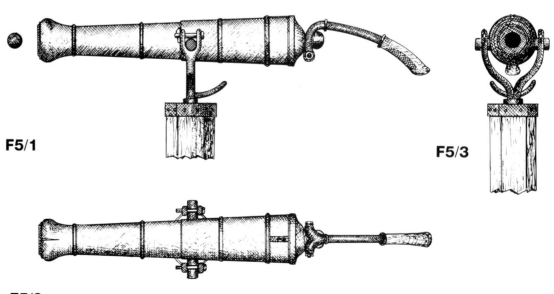

F5/1

F5/2

F5/3

G Masts and yards

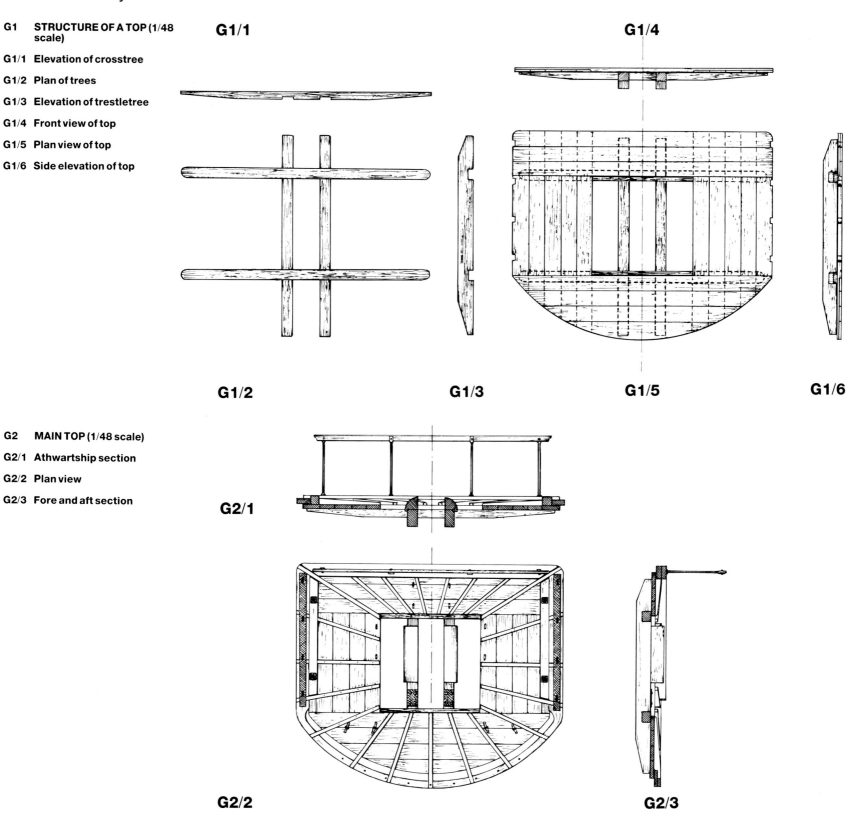

G1 STRUCTURE OF A TOP (1/48 scale)

G1/1 Elevation of crosstree

G1/2 Plan of trees

G1/3 Elevation of trestletree

G1/4 Front view of top

G1/5 Plan view of top

G1/6 Side elevation of top

G2 MAIN TOP (1/48 scale)

G2/1 Athwartship section

G2/2 Plan view

G2/3 Fore and aft section

G1/1

G1/4

G1/2

G1/3

G1/5

G1/6

G2/1

G2/2

G2/3

G Masts and yards

G3/1

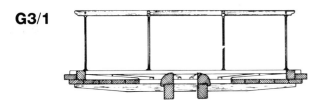

G3/2

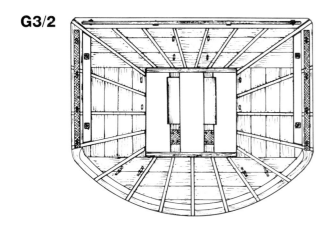

G4/1

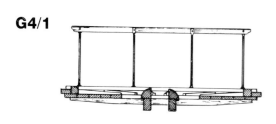

G4/2

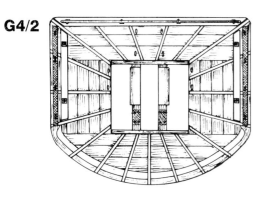

G3   **FORE TOP (1/58 scale)**

G3/1   **Athwartship section**

G3/2   **Plan view**

G4   **MIZZEN TOP (1/48 scale)**

G4/1   **Athwartship section**

G4/2   **Plan view**

G5   **MAIN TOP DETAILS (1/24 scale)**
The main top with the iron plate for the
futtock chainplates, the chock for
swivel guns, the lantern and the bolts
that fastened the top to the
trestletrees and crosstrees. Note the
iron plate on the trestletree where the
topmast fid rested.

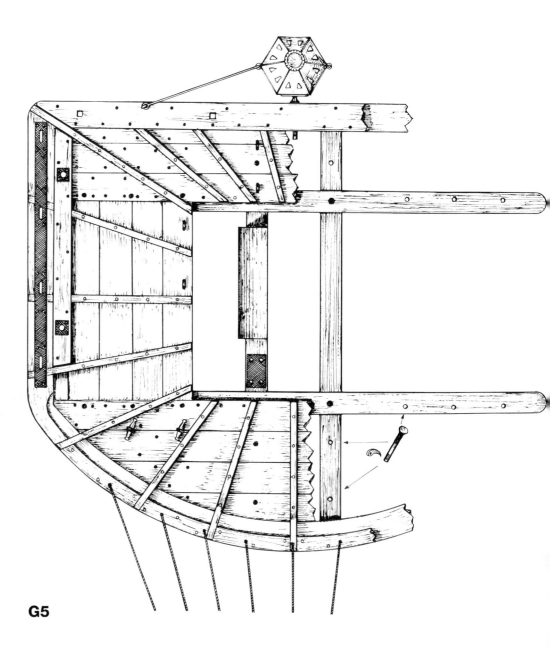

G5

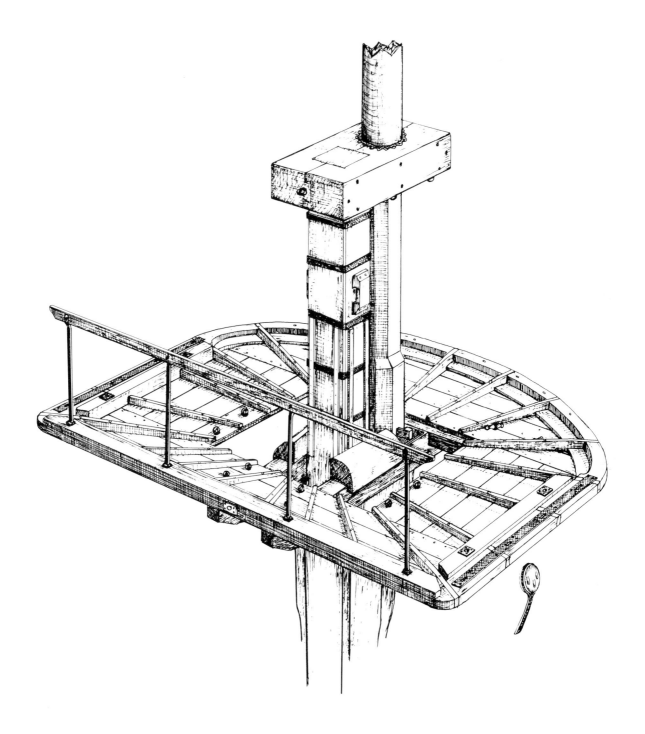

G6

G Masts and yards

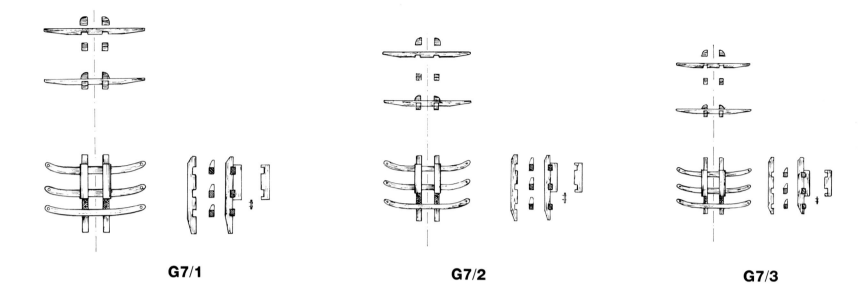

G7/1 **G7/2** **G7/3**

G7 **TOPMAST TRESTLETREES AND CROSSTREES (1/48 scale)**

G7/1 Main

G7/2 Fore

G7/3 Mizzen

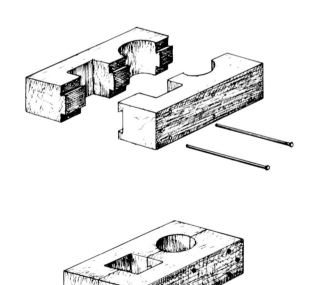

G8/7

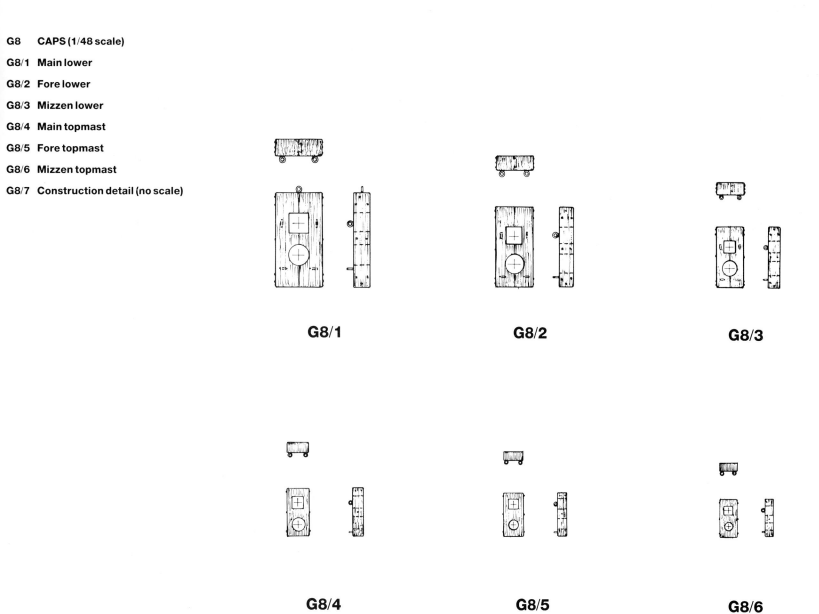

G8/1   **G8/2**   **G8/3**

G8/4   **G8/5**   **G8/6**

G Masts and yards

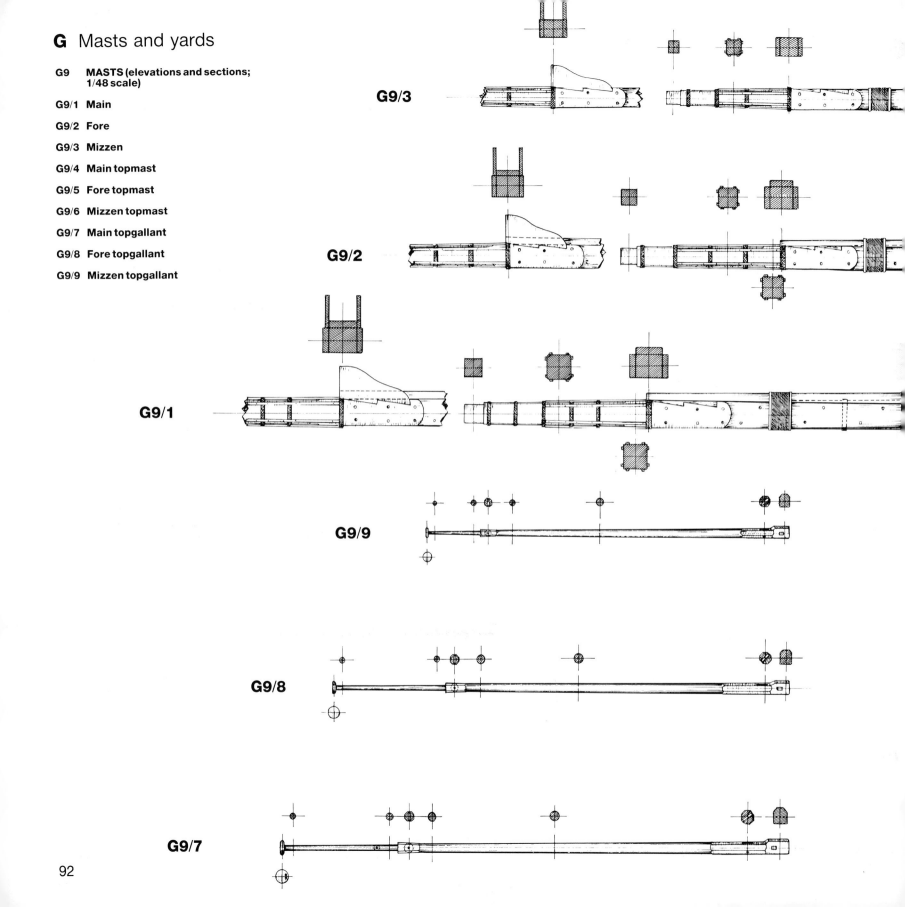

G9/3

G9/2

G9/1

G9/9

G9/8

G9/7

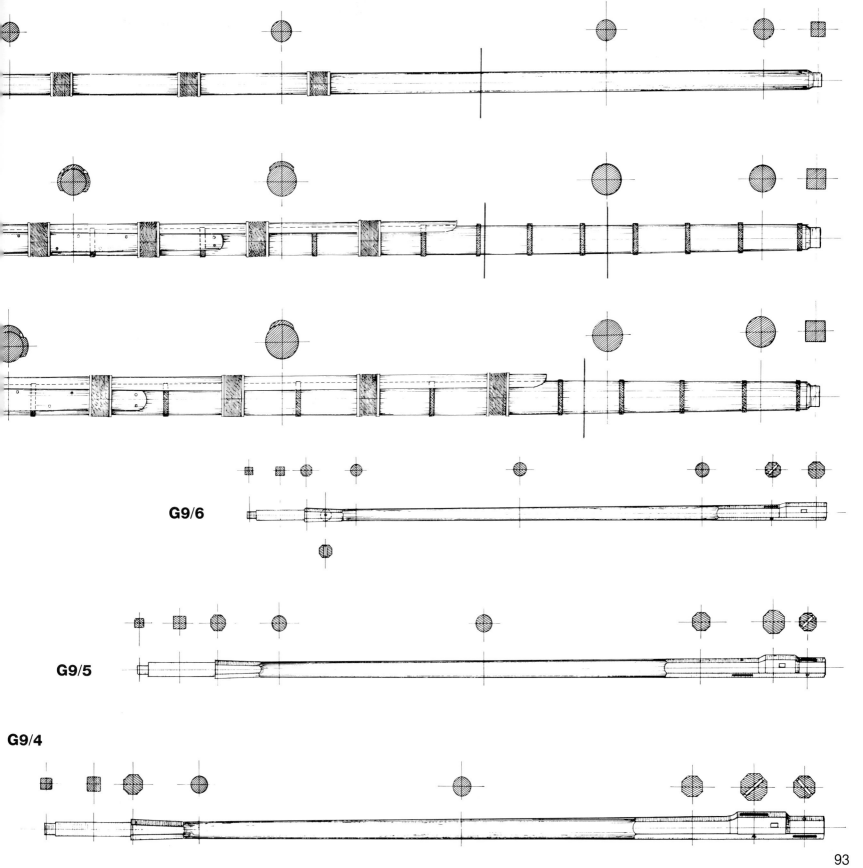

G9/6

G9/5

G9/4

G Masts and yards

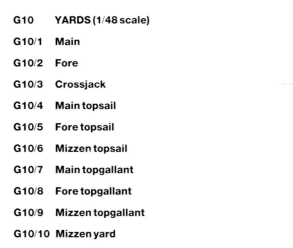

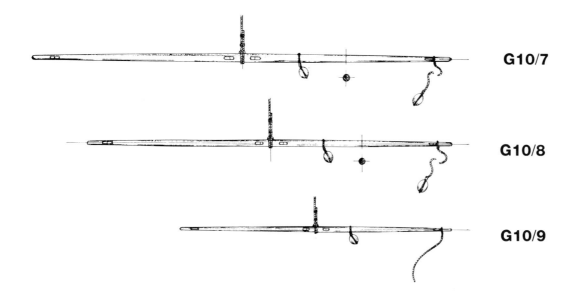

G10/7

G10/8

G10/9

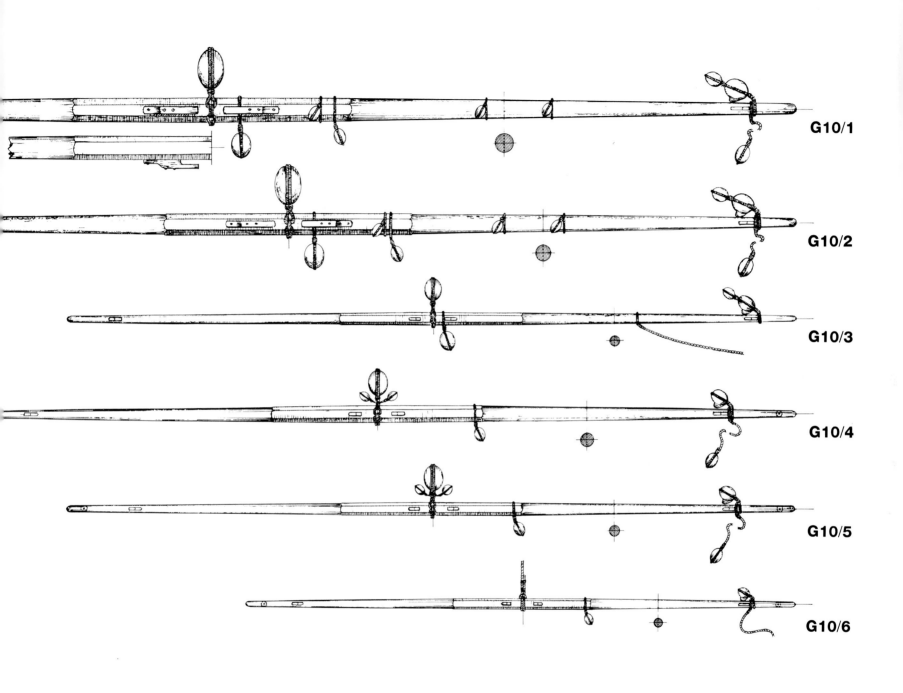

G10/1

G10/2

G10/3

G10/4

G10/5

G10/6

G10/10

G11/1

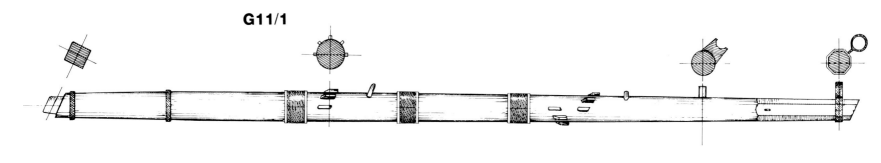

G11/3

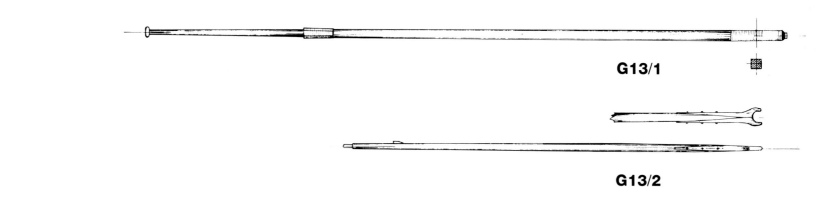

G13/1

G13/2

G13/4

G13/3

G11/2

G11/4

G11/5

G11/6

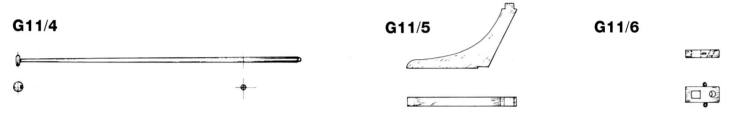

G11   **BOWSPRIT AND YARDS (1/48 scale)**

G11/1 **Bowsprit**

G11/2 **Jib boom**

G11/3 **Spritsail yard**

G11/4 **Jackstaff**

G11/5 **Knee for jackstaff**

G11/6 **Bowsprit cap**

G12   **ENSIGN STAFF (1/48 scale)**

G12

G13   **BOAT MAST AND SPARS (1/48 scale)**

G13/1 **Mast**

G13/2 **Boom**

G13/3 **Gaff**

G13/4 **Ensign staff**

H Rigging and sails

H1 STANDING RIGGING (1/192 scale)
For rigging identification numbers see
table of keys on p100

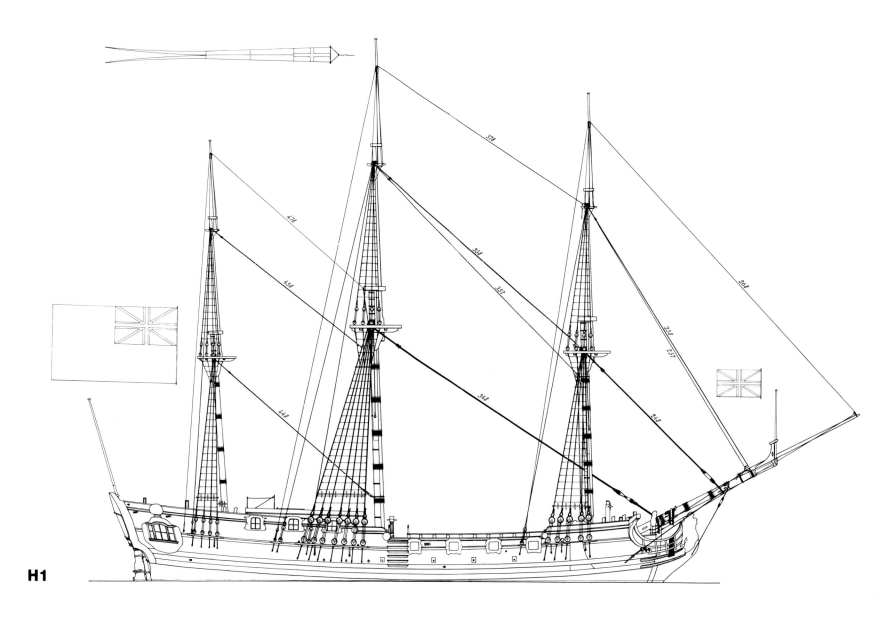

H1

H2 CHAINWALE AND DEADEYES
(1/24 scale)

H2/1 Elevation

H2/2 Athwartship section
The shroud cable is four-strand, cable laid. The method of making the bight which held the deadeye is described in the text. The seizings are in the order one throat seizing and two round seizings. The second (upper) seizing was done, according to Steel, using a finer rope than the other two.

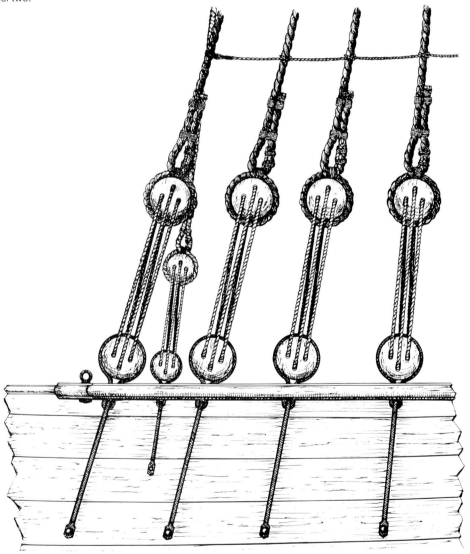

H2/1

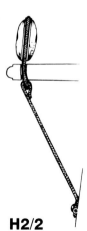

H2/2

H Rigging and sails

H3   DEADEYES (1/12 scale)

H3/1 Upper (shroud) deadeye

H3/2 Lower (chain) deadeye

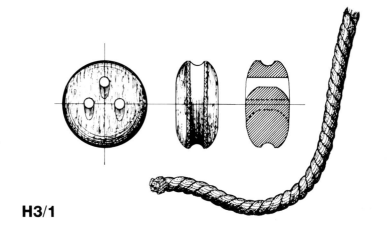

H3/1

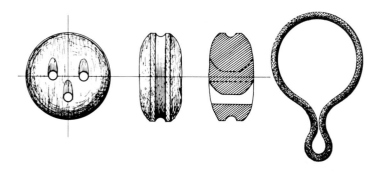

H3/2

RIGGING KEY

Course	Spritsail	Fore	Main	Mizzen
Jeers (or tie/halyard)	111	211	311	–
Lift	112	212	312	412
Parrel (or slings to spritsail)	113	213	313	413
Brace	114	214	314	414
Sheet	115	215	315	–
Clueline	116	216	316	–
Buntline	117	217	317	–
Leechline	–	218	318	–
Bowline	–	219	319	–
Tack	–	210	310	–

Topsails		Fore	Main	Mizzen
Tie/halyard		221	321	421
Lift		222	322	422
Parrel		223	323	423
Brace		224	324	424
Sheet		225	325	425
Clueline		226	326	426
Buntline		227	327	427
Leechline		228	328	428
Bowline		229	329	429
Reef tackle		220	320	420

Topgallant sails		Fore	Main	Mizzen
Tie/halyard		231	331	431
Lift		232	332	432
Parrel		233	333	433
Brace		234	334	434
Sheet*		–	–	–
Clueline		236	336	436
Bowline		239	339	439

  * see topsail lift

Staysails		Fore	Main	Mizzen
Lower staysail				
Halyard		–	–	441
Sheet		–	–	445
Tack		–	–	440
Downhauler		–	–	449
Stay		248	348	448
Topsail staysail				
Halyard		251	351	451
Sheet		255	355	455
Tack		250	350	450
Downhauler		259	359	459
Staysail stay		257	357	–
Stay		258	358	458
Jib				
Halyard		261		
Sheet		265		
Tack		260		
Downhauler		269		
Inhauler		269a		
Outhauler		269b		
Staysail stay		267		

Mizzen sail				Mizzen
Halyard				481
Mizzen lift				482
Mizzen parrel				483
Vang				484
Sheet				485
Brails				486
Bowline				489

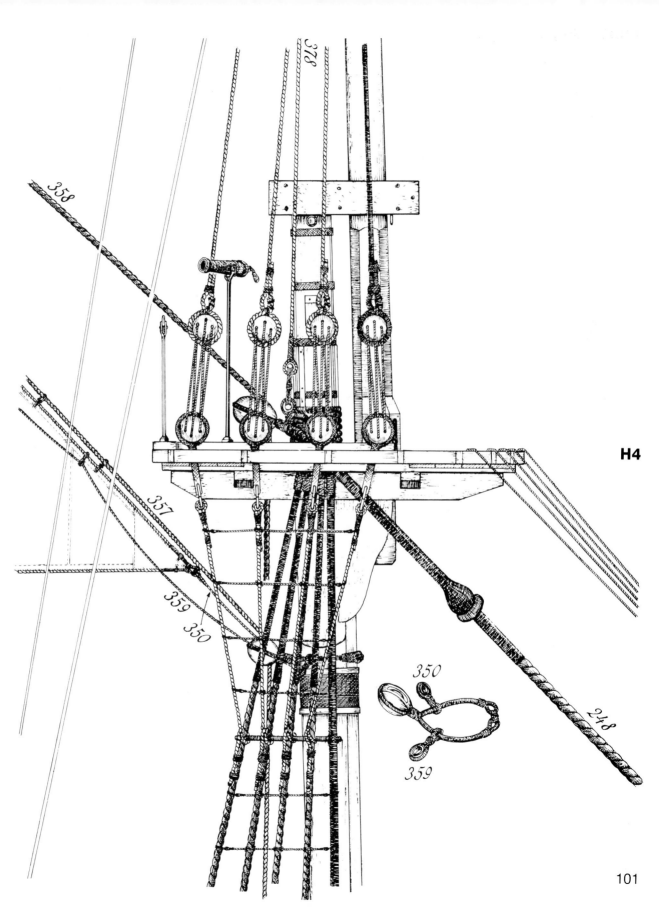

H4 **RIGGING AT THE FORE TOP (1/24 scale)**
Note the forestay; the fore rim of the top carries the holes for the crowsfeet, which prevented the topsail from chafing and fouling against the platform

378

358

357

359 350

350

359

248

H4

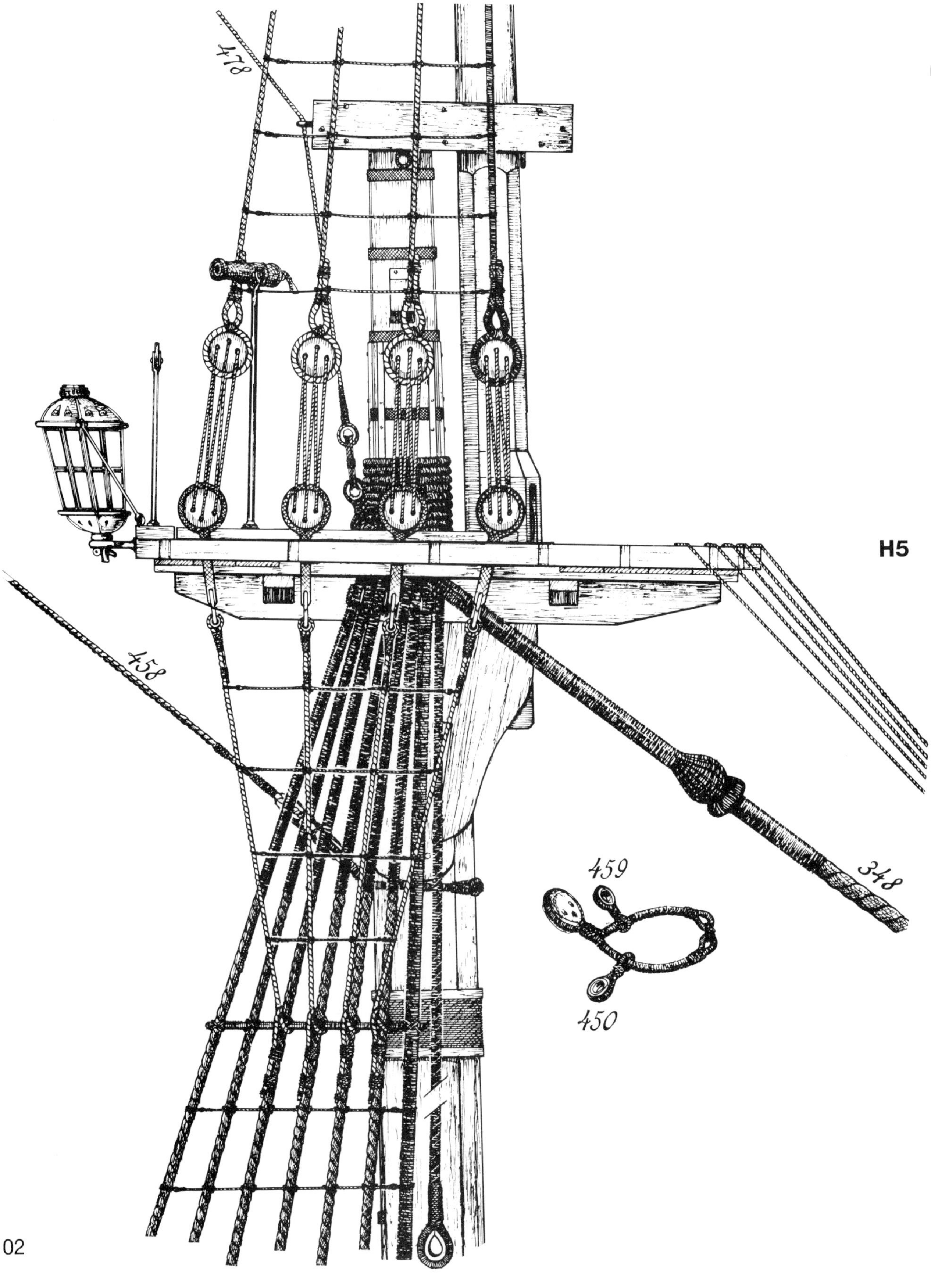

478

**H5   STANDING RIGGING AT THE
      MAIN TOP (1/24 scale)**
Note the stanchion with half-pound
swivel gun and the topmast lantern.
The mizzen topgallant stay is set up
with two thimbles on the main collar
stay while the mizzen topmast stay is
set up with deadeyes on its collar
under the top.

H5

458

348

459

450

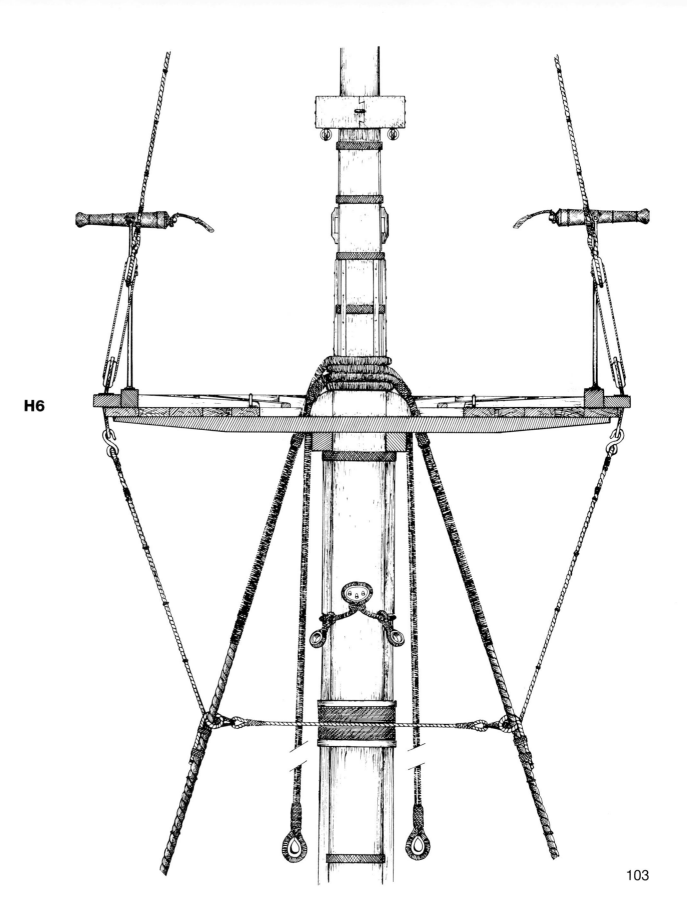

**H6   MAINMAST FROM ABAFT
SHOWING THE CATHARPINS
(1/24 scale)**

H6

482

H7

486

486

486

448

447

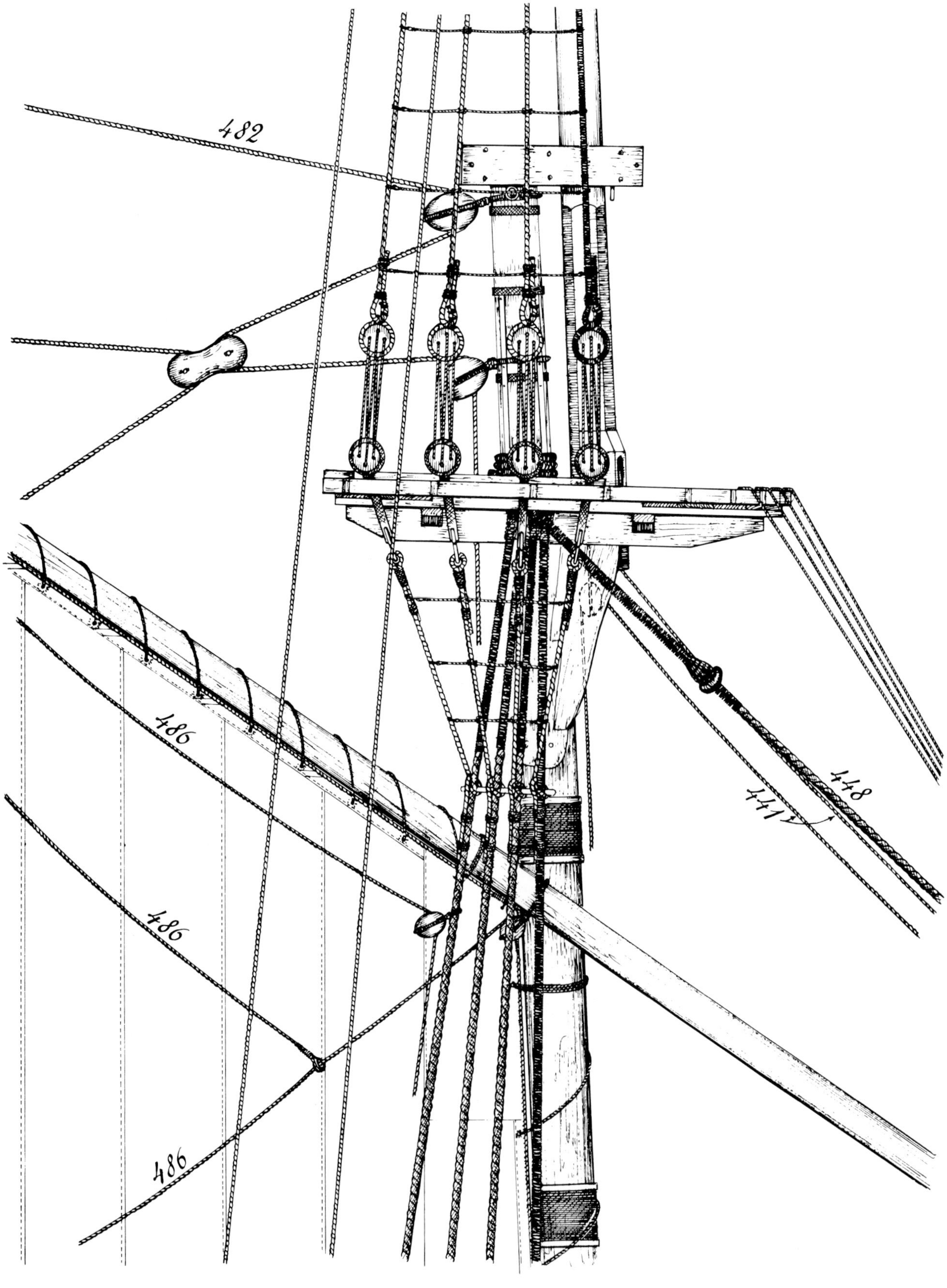

H8 FORE TOPMAST (1/24 scale)
Note the cheek blocks bolted at the head of the mast

H8/1 Side elevation

H8/2 View from aft

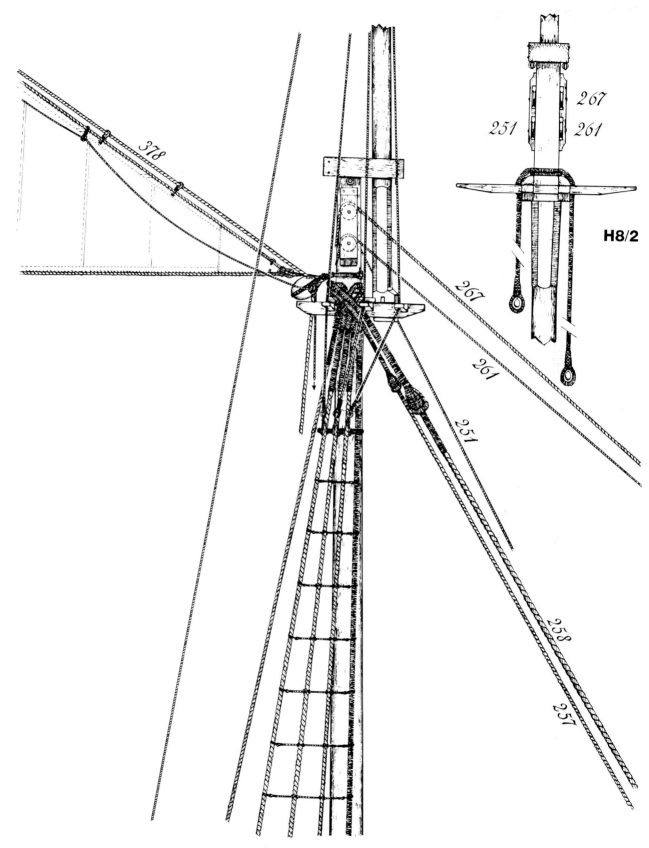

H8/1

H8/2

H Rigging and sails

H9   MAIN TOPMAST HEAD (1/24 scale)

H9/1   Side elevation

H9/2   View from aft
Showing how the topgallant shrouds were set up. There were no catharpins

H9/1

H9/2

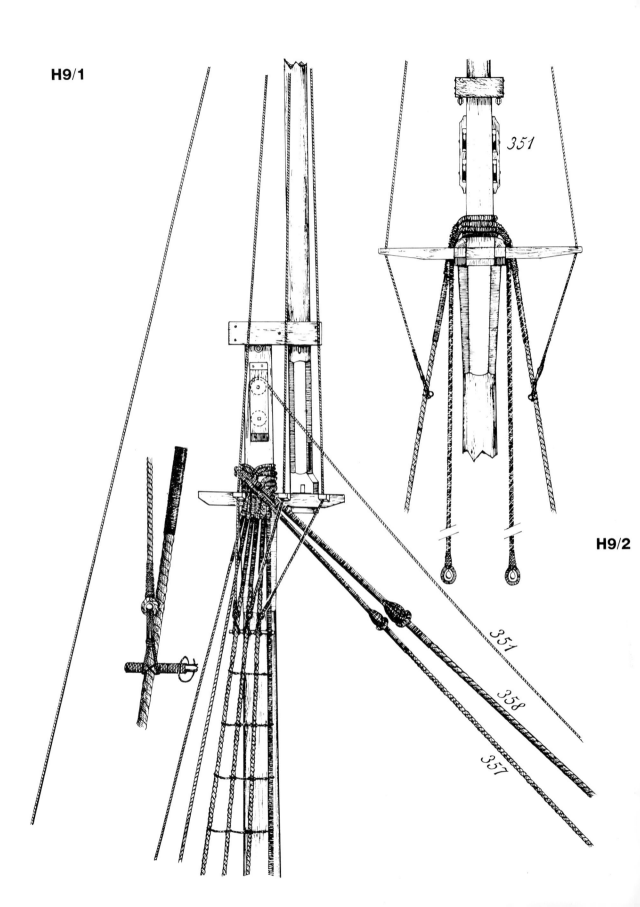

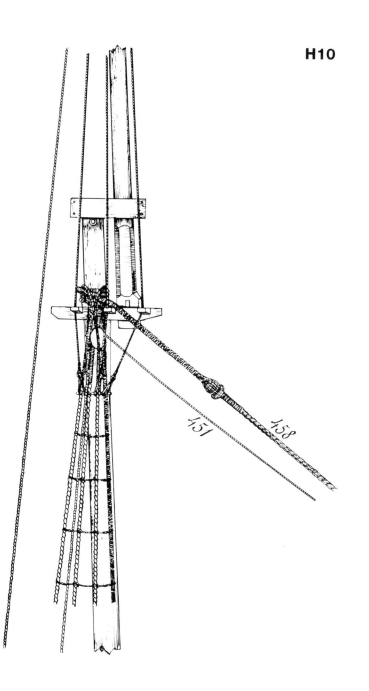

H10

H10   MIZZEN TOPMAST HEAD (1/24 scale)

H11   PERSPECTIVE VIEW OF TOP WITH TIE OF THE YARD (no scale)
There is no proof for ships of this period, but when a battle was expected there ought to have been some system for blocking the tie so that it did not run through the blocks if damaged; chain or rope slings came into official use after 1773.

451   458

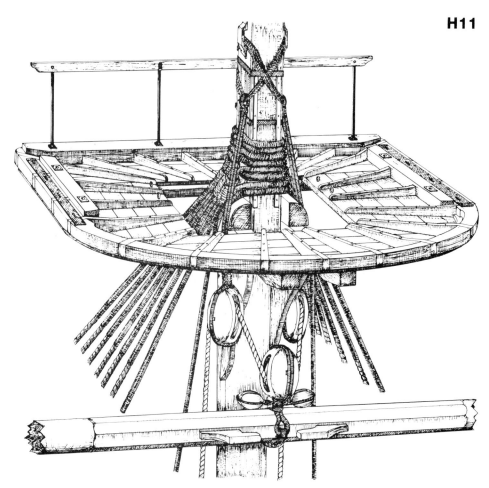

H11

H Rigging and sails

H12   HALYARDS OF THE COURSES
       (1/24 scale)

H12/1   Side elevation

H12/2   View from forward

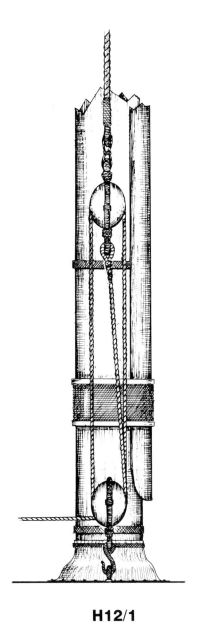

H12/1

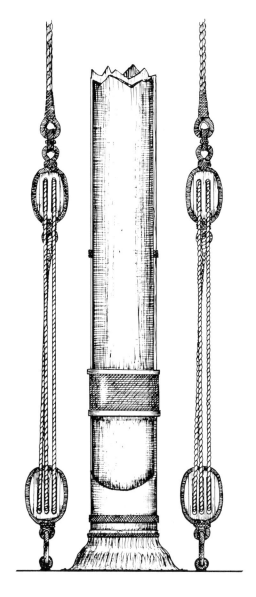

H12/2

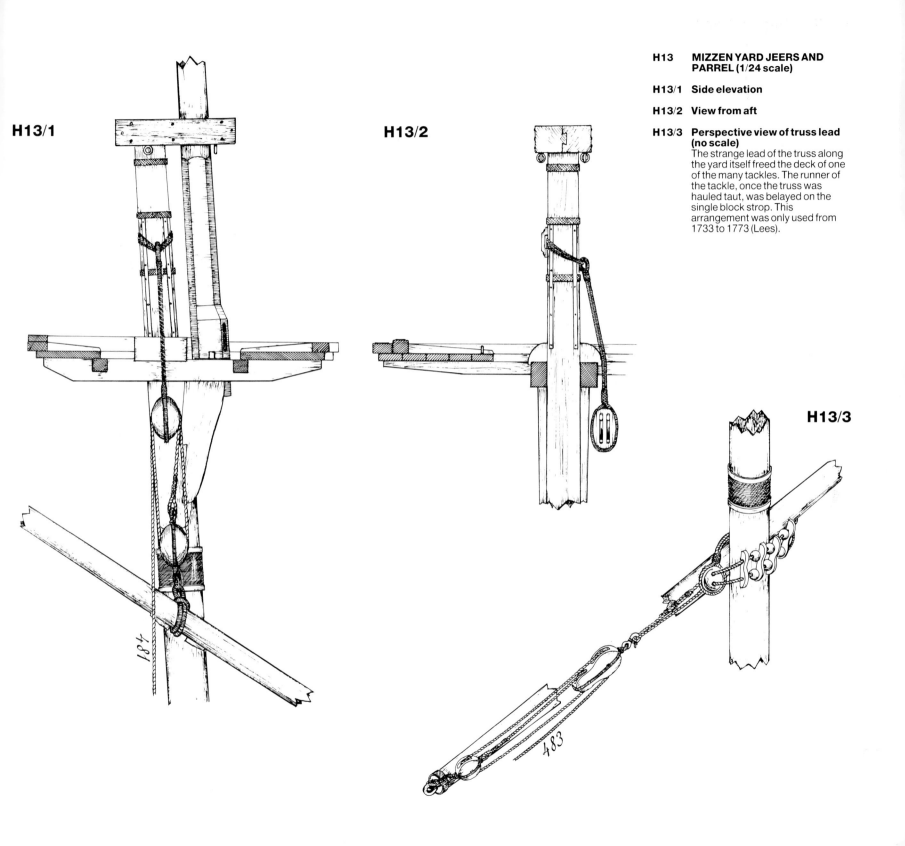

H13/1

H13/2

H13   MIZZEN YARD JEERS AND
       PARREL (1/24 scale)

H13/1 Side elevation

H13/2 View from aft

H13/3 Perspective view of truss lead
       (no scale)

The strange lead of the truss along
the yard itself freed the deck of one
of the many tackles. The runner of
the tackle, once the truss was
hauled taut, was belayed on the
single block strop. This
arrangement was only used from
1733 to 1773 (Lees).

H13/3

481

483

109

H14 MAIN TOPSAIL TIE (no scale)
showing how the long strop of the
blocks and the standing part of the tie
were seized to the masthead.

**H15 DETAIL OF A TOPSAIL PARREL
(no scale)**

H15

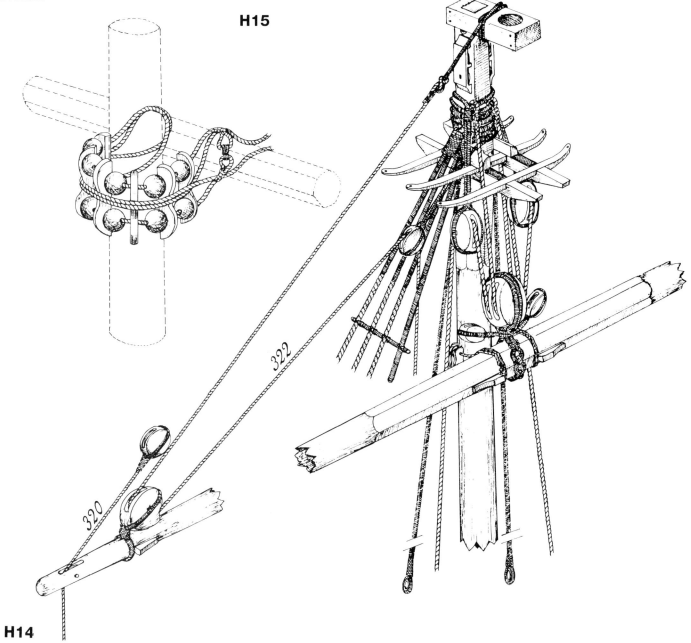

322

320

H14

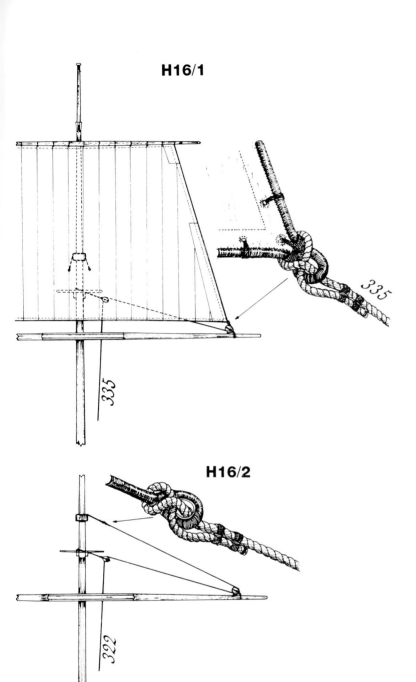

H16/1

335

335

H16/2

322

322

H16 **TOPGALLANT SHEET (no scale)**

H16/1 **With sail set**

H16/2 **With topgallant furled**

H16/3 **Cap pendant**
The topgallant sheet at main, fore and mizzen acted as a topsail lift as well. When the topgallant sail was taken in, the rope was seized to the pendant at the cap.

H17 **CROSSJACK SLINGS AND TRUSS (1/24 scale)**

H17/1 **The crossjack slings**
This is not a tie; it is not too clear why the slings were rigged with a block as in this figure.

H17/2 **Detail of the crossjack truss**
This was used instead of parrels.

H16/3

322

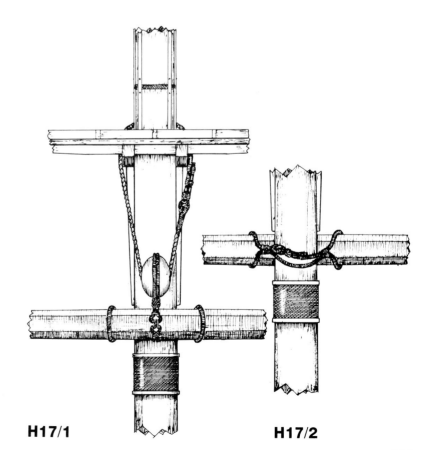

H17/1 **H17/2**

H18 SQUARE SAILS (1/192 scale)

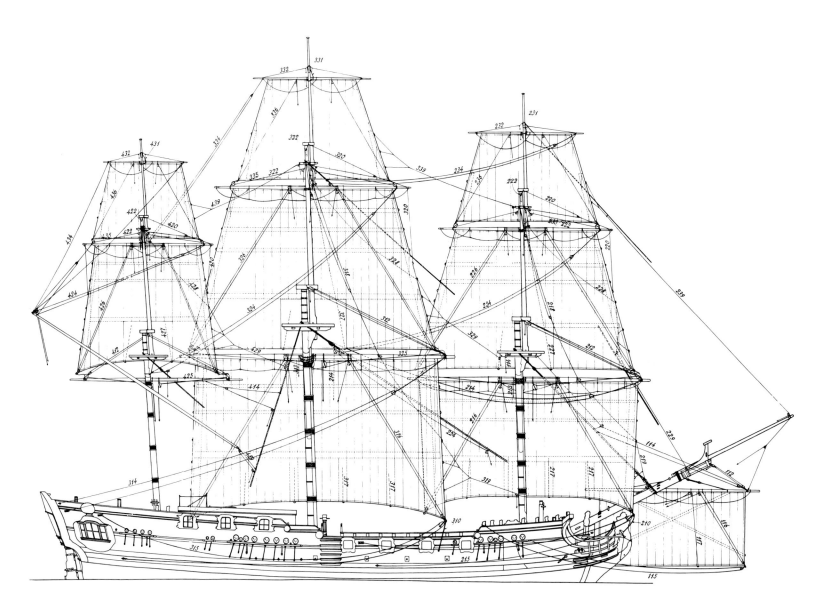

H18

H19　FORE AND AFT SAILS (1/192 scale)

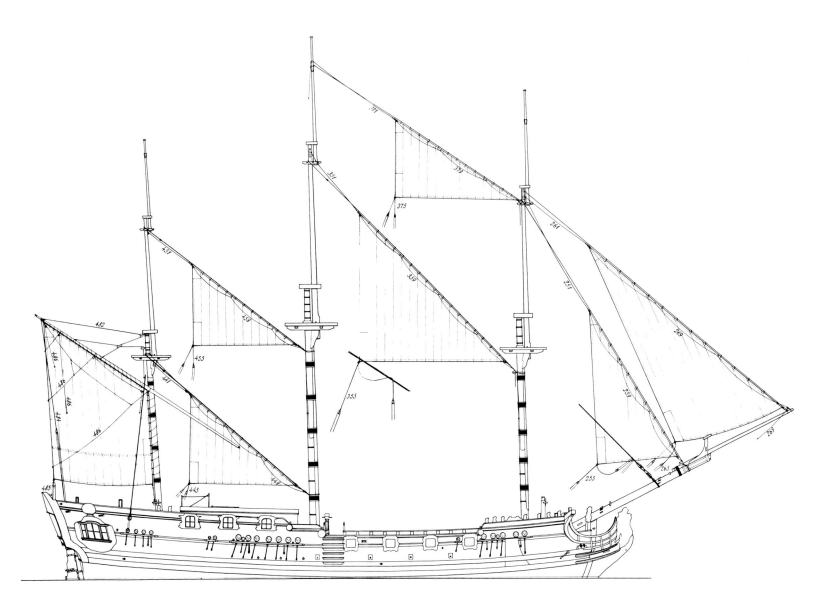

H19

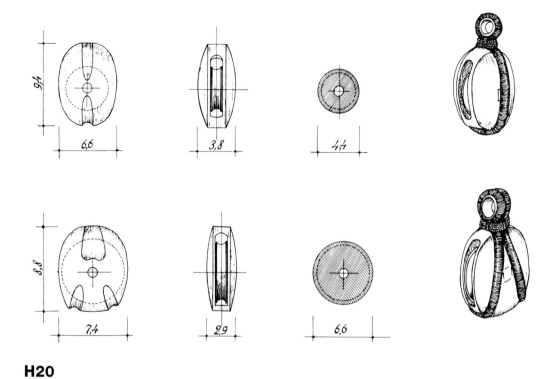

H20

The measurements of normal blocks (above) and flat thin blocks (below). Using a flat block meant that a double block or a long-tackle could be eliminated. Their weight and the weight of the rope fall, constantly swinging, wore against and strained the topmasts. The sheave of the flat thin block was bigger and compensated for the loss of mechanical advantage due to the elimination of the long-tackle block.

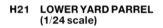

H21 LOWER YARD PARREL
(1/24 scale)

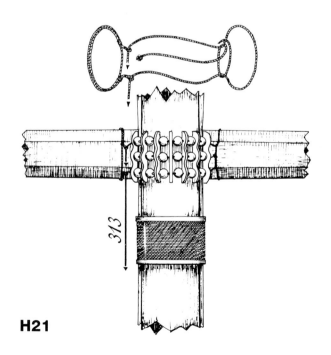

H21

H22   YARDARM TACKLE (1/48 scale)

When not in use, it was hooked to the futtock stave. The tackle was used for a lot of heavy duty operations such as raising and lowering the ship's boats. The tricing line made fast on the top was used to bring the tackle into the desired position.

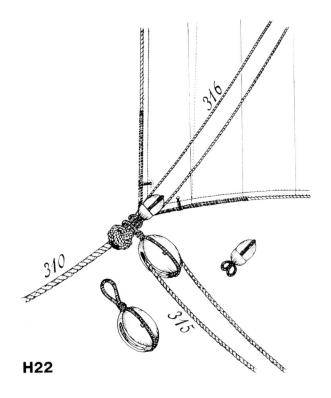

H22

H23   CLUE OF A COURSE (no scale)

Note the sheet block, the special block for the clueline (a shoulder block) and the tack, secured to the clue of the sail by the big tack knot at its end.

H23

H24

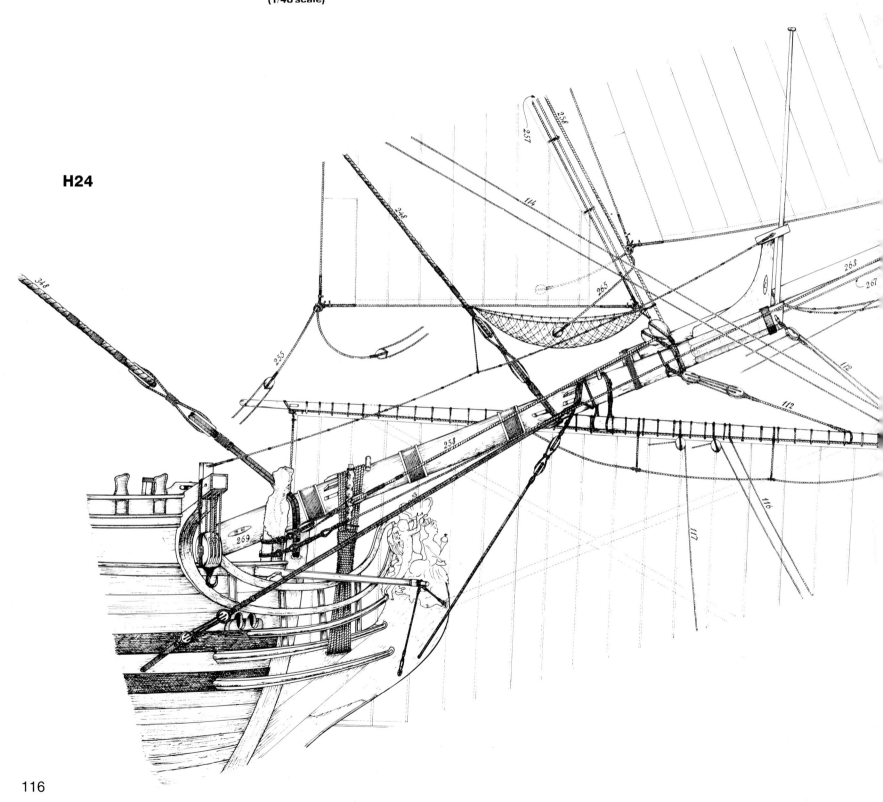

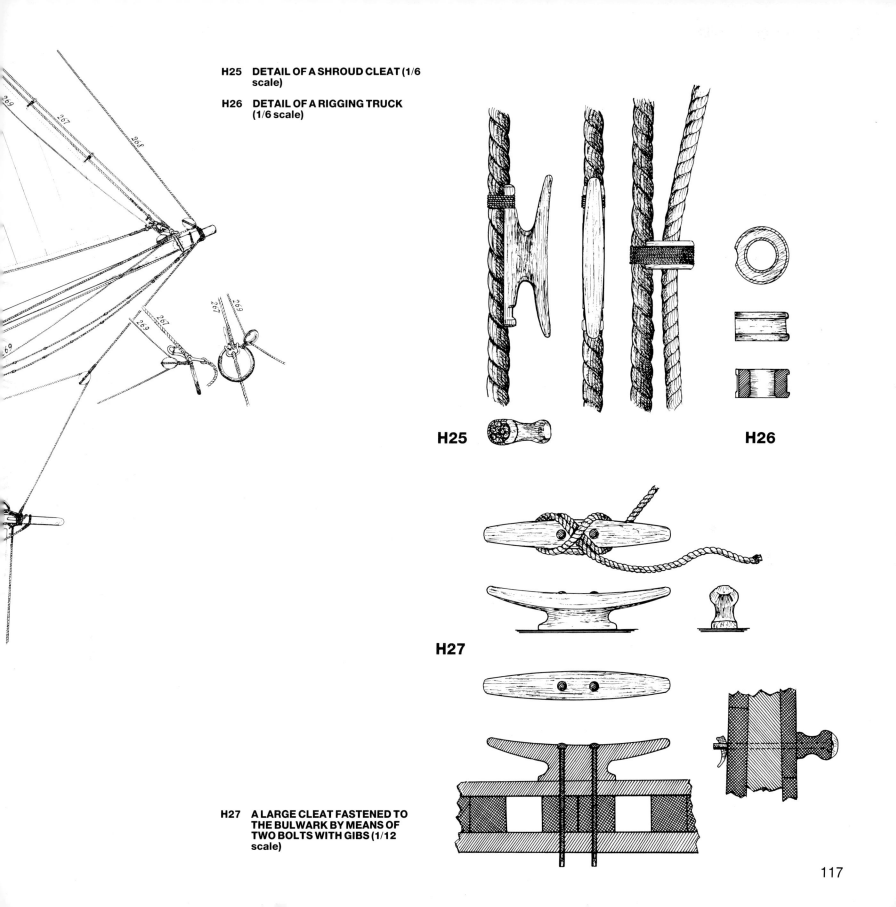

H25 DETAIL OF A SHROUD CLEAT (1/6 scale)

H26 DETAIL OF A RIGGING TRUCK (1/6 scale)

H25

H26

H27

H27 A LARGE CLEAT FASTENED TO THE BULWARK BY MEANS OF TWO BOLTS WITH GIBS (1/12 scale)

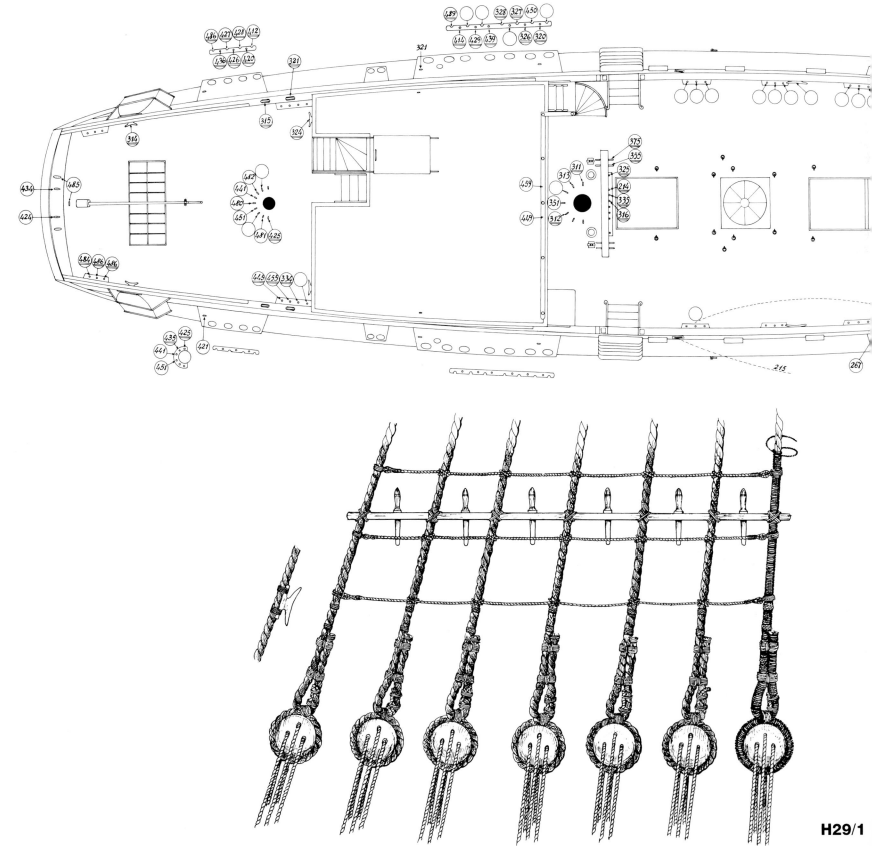

118

H29/1

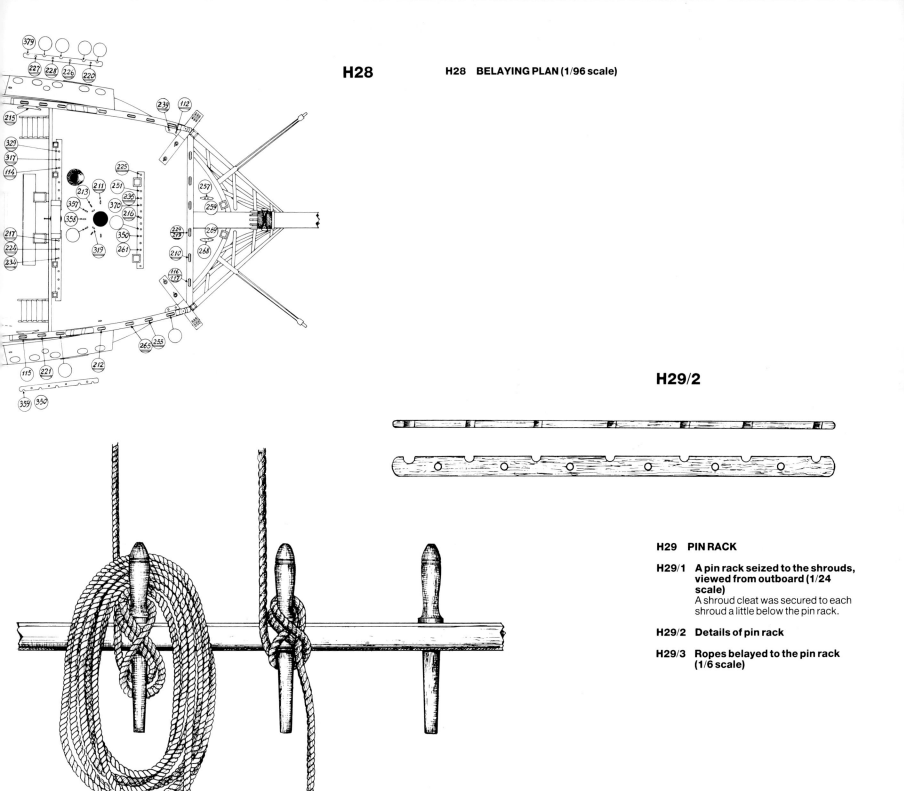

H28   H28   BELAYING PLAN (1/96 scale)

H29/2

H29   PIN RACK

H29/1   **A pin rack seized to the shrouds,
viewed from outboard (1/24
scale)**
A shroud cleat was secured to each
shroud a little below the pin rack.

H29/2   **Details of pin rack**

H29/3   **Ropes belayed to the pin rack
(1/6 scale)**

H29/3

H Rigging and sails

H30   **BELAYING POINTS ON THE TOPS AND ON THE BITTS (no scale)**

H30/1   **Main jeer bitts**

H30/2   **Fore jeer bitts**

H30/3   **Mizzen top**

H30/4   **Main top**

H30/5   **Fore top**

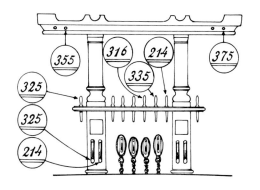

H30/1

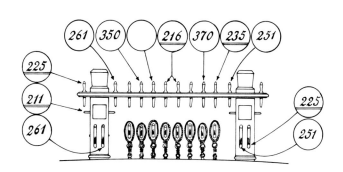

H30/2

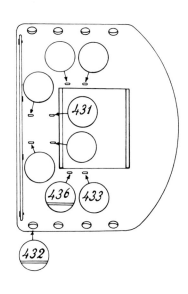

H30/3

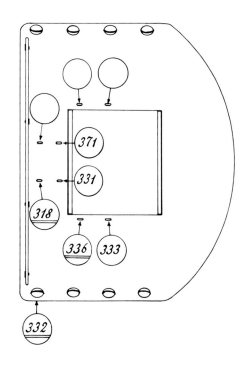

H30/4

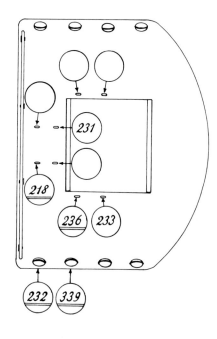

H30/5